MAESTRO

MATTERS

BY

PAMELA JAY MA

Published in June 2010 by emp3books Ltd
Kiln Workshops, Pilcot Road, Crookham Village,
Fleet, Hampshire, GU51 5RY, England

©Pamela Jay 2010

The author asserts the moral right to be identified as the
author of this work. All views are those of the author.

ISBN-13: 978-1-907140-11-2

DEDICATION.

To Nigel and Anthony Jay, for their help and guidance.

ACKNOWLEDGEMENTS.

Special thanks to my photographer colleagues, Tom Bangbala, Andrew Price and John Wade, without whom the book would have lost an extra dimension; Günther Herbig for originally encouraging me to publish; Alan Dunn (ex-Guardian journalist) for correcting my grammatical errors; Sir Peter Maxwell Davies for correcting errors in the text; John Smale for the production assistance; the financial support of the Ida Carroll Trust in association with the Manchester Musical Heritage Trust and finally all the musicians, conductors and colleagues who have willingly or unwittingly contributed to this book.

FOREWORD

It is a great privilege to introduce Pamela Jay's book about life in a professional orchestra in general, and about the players' relationship with conductors in particular.

Her story is as frank and honest as such a tale could ever be – full of both delicious sly humour and serious, penetrating insight. It is a moving book, too – one becomes very aware of the extremely close camaraderie inside the orchestra, as well as being mightily impressed by the members' love for music in common. The collective determination to get things right, and to do one's upmost in the cause of good music-making is both reassuring and inspiring.

The interviews with conductors are sympathetic and sensitive, and ring absolutely true - never too deferential, and always informed with a real understanding of the difficulties of the craft. Ms. Jay has encouraged her interviewees to express insights invaluable to anyone interested in conducting – from the point of view of a would-be conductor, a potential orchestral musician, and, indeed, of a listener who just cares passionately about music.

I only wish I had had the opportunity to read this book before I ever conducted an orchestra! Every page made me smile with the pleasure of recognition – yes, that is exactly how it is!

Sir Peter Maxwell Davies,
Master of the Queen's Music

INTRODUCTION

From an early age, I have been obsessed with everything and anything to do with music. Music was my life, my raison d'être. Having started to work through all the grades on the piano, I realised that, as much as I liked the piano, I was not cut out to be a soloist - I needed to feel part of a group. Playing the piano excited me tremendously, but I couldn't envisage a career doing this and nothing else. The death of my piano teacher occurred unexpectedly just before my final exam, and brought home to me that my goals in life would suddenly have to change. My father, who calmly surveyed the situation, secretly unearthed a rather sorry version of a violin in the attic one day, carelessly leaving it propped up in the corner of the lounge. As he expected, curiosity took over and I scraped away in a vain attempt to produce something satisfying. He took the instrument to a local music shop for an overhaul and proudly returned with a superior model under his arm. Starting again through the grades was a challenge; I could only have lessons on one thing at a time so I tried to keep the piano going as best I could. I joined the local youth orchestra and led two visits to Germany; was invited to join the ranks of a string orchestra made up of local freelancers who wanted to perform in churches and halls for their own pleasure; and gradually I was transformed from the insular pianist to the enthusiastic orchestral player. At my audition for the college orchestra, the conductor put some sight-reading in front of me. 'I had to look really hard for something I thought you hadn't played before!" He was absolutely right. Granville Bantock's 'Fifine at the Fair' was a piece I truly hadn't seen before or ever again for that matter!

I joined D'Oyly Carte for a while, playing violin at night and working with the chorus during the day, which was most enjoyable. However, I dearly wanted a place in the BBC Philharmonic, then called the BBC Northern Symphony Orchestra. One finally became available in 1972 and remarkably there are still a few of us in the band who joined at a similar time. I have journeyed from nearly the youngest female in the band to the most senior, though not necessarily the most mature! My future husband was invited to join a few years after me, having also progressed via D'Oyly Carte, and we both feel it a privilege to be involved with musical matters day in day out. Apart from the orchestra, there is always some project on the go – string quartet and chamber music concerts to organise; youth orchestras to coach; former pupils to keep in touch with; present ones to be encouraged…there just aren't enough hours in the day!

However, there are always two sides to a coin. If you experience the highs you are bound to find the lows. When all performers on stage are charged up together and all responding to the information sent by the conductor, then there is nothing like it in the world. Conversely, when you as a group are desperately trying to battle against an incoherent or indifferent conductor, then you feel that all the years of your training have been wasted. If the conductor appears to be not in control of the hundred minds in front of him, then the life and soul is taken from the performance - depression and frustration taking their place. As long as this is the exception then we can cope, but what if there is a lack of inspiration from the conductors of the future? How can we as players survive, mentally and physically? What on earth will the orchestras of the future have to look forward to? Their existence lies in the hands of so few!

1st Mov. : ALLEGRO MODERATO
From orchestra to podium

Most orchestral rehearsals begin in a similar fashion. Players assemble their instrument, music, pencils and erasers whilst busily chatting over the merits of the previous night's concert or difficulty of getting into work by bus, train, cycle, car etc. There is always a general buzz of activity before the leader walks in and requests an 'A' from the oboe. The atmosphere slowly changes as minds begin to focus on the work in hand – whatever the management has organised on the schedule for that morning. Fears and hopes for the following three hours have been exchanged, the new conductor has been introduced and welcomed by a staff member, the height and position of the podium has been adjusted to his satisfaction, and the conductor raises his baton. So far so good, you would think. However, the conductor is a newcomer to the orchestra's home territory. He is the stranger, the visitor, and the invited guest – invited of course by the management, who will disappear to their offices as soon as the down beat falls and all orchestral members have been counted as present and correct. What happens for the next session becomes a bone of contention if the players' fears are not allayed, and they start worrying how they are going to survive the week without feeling completely drained of the enthusiasm they, at present, might have for the music before them.

Although it is a well known fact within musical circles that orchestral musicians will have made up their minds about the new conductor during the first few minutes in the studio, I can understand that it can be a frightening thought for the new conductor walking into a room full of strangers who have worked together for years and know each other's foibles. Some say that the way a conductor walks into the room and up to the podium will decide the fate of the following rehearsal. Not a word is spoken, yet the general feeling will spread like Chinese whispers. This phenomenon is not a new one; even the age of the prospective newcomer has been a bone of contention for decades, as Bernard Shore (one time principal viola in the BBC Symphony Orchestra), describes so well in his book 'The Orchestra Speaks', written in the 1930s. Even in those days he says conductors under the age of 35 or 40 were not welcomed by top orchestras, because the players resented being criticised by someone who thought he knew everything and yet still had to prove his worth. If he talked very little and showed some humility he got on best!

In 1922, Richard Strauss found it necessary to produce Ten Golden Rules for Young Conductors:

1. Remember that you are making music not to amuse yourself but to delight your audience.
2. You should not perspire when conducting; only the audience should get warm.
3. Conduct Salome and Elektra as if they were Mendelssohn's 'Fairy Music'.
4. Never look encouragingly at the brass, except with a short glance to give them an important cue.
5. But never let the horns and woodwind out of your sight: if you can hear them at all, they are too strong.
6. If you think the brass is blowing hard enough, tone it down a shade or two.
7. It is not enough that you yourself should hear every word the soloist sings – you know it off by heart anyway; the audience must be able to follow without effort. If they do not understand the words, they will go to sleep.
8. Always accompany a singer in such a way that he can sing without effort.
9. When you think you have reached the limits of prestissimo. Double the pace.
10. If you follow these rules carefully you will, with your fine gifts and your great accomplishments, always be the darling of your listeners.[1]

---

[1] Jan Younghusband, *Orchestra,* (Chatto & Windus Ltd., 1991) 194

At this point in the game the players will still be divided in their opinions. They have not yet had time to discuss their feelings openly, but if something is amiss - a peculiar tempo, an unsteady one, anything at all- then a few raised eyebrows will be exchanged either by desk partners or across the room. Remember that many violinists look up from the music and immediately face cellists, viewing the conductor at an angle, from out the corner of an eye. So any rehearsal atmosphere will be strained, at least until the break time if not the whole day. It often takes a coffee break to dispel some fears or air some opinions for the general atmosphere to settle down and players to accept their fate as best they can.

Max Rudolph describes a conductor as *'part musician, part actor'* in his treatise, 'The Grammar of Conducting'. He also states that when speaking of a 'born surgeon' no one would suggest that a medical person, no matter how brilliant, should take charge of an operation unless he was thoroughly trained in the theory and practice of his craft. Riccardo Muti put it a different way: 'A conductor is only a bridge between music and the public. If he draws too much attention to himself by what he is doing technically, externally, rather than trying to communicate the inner musical content of the work, he fails the music. He can do no more than transmit his mental image of a work to the players. He can no longer *impose* his will, because the days of dictatorial conductors are over. Yet at the crucial moment when a conductor first comes into contact with an orchestra, it is not only the orchestra who judges the conductor; he, too, instantly forms an opinion of its capacities and potential, and this is partly why this first moment in which the two forces judge each other is so full of suspense; each studies the other and tries to guess what kettle of fish he will shortly be dealing with. A great number of things are decided at that first contact. Sometimes, it determines whether a concert will be good or not.'[2]

Another aspect of conducting that is so important to the players is to know what to say and when to say it, when to criticise

[2] Helena Matheopoulos, *Maestro*, (Hutchinson Publishing Group, 1982) 360,361,363

and when to give encouragement. Sometimes a joke will lighten the atmosphere in the room ready for another bout of intense concentration. All these things have to be judged correctly if the conductor wants to build up a good rapport with his newly found colleagues. There has to be a mutual respect, but this has to be earned and there are no textbooks to explain how it can happen. Bernard Haitink's advice was not to use five words when two would do. 'In fact the amount you can show with your hands is amazing and conductors who tend to talk a lot should remember that at the concert itself they cannot talk at all. Don't display any signs of egomania, because orchestras hate it. Of course, you must have the ability to communicate and the gift of inspiring the players, but this should only be done spontaneously. You shouldn't spoil this by showing off, because orchestral players have a terrific instinct for what is real and what isn't. Just by the way a man picks up his stick and turns the pages, the orchestra can feel whether he has personality – yes or no." [3]

There has to be some give and take like any successful relationship – too much control and the players become subordinate, too little control and the orchestra will produce their own performance, similar to the one they gave for the previous conductor, however long ago that might have been. The Australian Steve Irwin was remarkable in his rapport with wild animals; he could get so close to the crocodiles yet be very aware that they could suddenly turn on him and eat him up in a second. Such was the thrill and excitement for him he constantly had to judge how far he could go and what reactions to expect. That nervousness was par for the course: he had to be one step ahead all the time and not show his inner fear. Surely there are some similarities here?

The amount of rehearsal time has always been a bone of contention - too much being as bad as too little. Even in 1938 Bernard Shore described how a conductor could either interest and thrill the orchestra or make players wish they were dead. You only had to look at the faces of the orchestral players to find out which it was to be. If they showed alertness and sparkle, then there was a

---

[3] Matheopoulos 203,205

man they could respect in front of them; if no one seemed to be interested in the stick or, in fact, anything at all, then the conductor was severely lacking in authority.

Orchestras are very aware that their future existence lies in the hands of the conductor. If the audience is not moved by the performance, however good the playing, then they might not return to the concert hall again should the same combination of conductor and orchestra appear in the future. Apparently, Toscanini was renowned for keeping rehearsals fresh and interesting so much so that rehearsals were looked forward to, everyone showing great concentration, and the rehearsal time just flew by.

To occupy the minds and imagination of a room full of people is no easy matter as conductors have to stop the flow of the music when something is not balanced right, or the orchestra is not reacting together to a change of tempo. There can be hundreds of reasons for this; however, spending minutes discussing the various possible bowings with a few front desks will take its toll on the rest of the band. Wind and brass players are not affected by bowings, often not needing pencils at all for most rehearsals, so their attention is going to be lost. Back desks aren't involved in the discussion either, even if it does eventually affect them. Then they have to wait patiently until a decision is made. The time taken to write the amended version in the copies either adds to the delay or causes frustration when the conductor begins rehearsing again while parts are still being adjusted. This is a balancing act all the time, and the conductor has to make a decision – occupy the brass to get them on board again, or let the string players do their stuff in already heavily over marked parts. Continually stopping the flow of the music every few bars is very irritating, especially when the movement of the baton alone should be sufficient enough to convey most emotions.

William Mendelberg preferred to have five rehearsals at his disposal for a symphony concert, four being sectionals, and only in the final rehearsal would he put all sections together. He would be no friend of either the management juggling finances, or players juggling boredom in the British orchestral scene of today. Rehearsals cost money as do concerts, and we all have to be geared up to make the best use of too little time. Rehearsal time is working time, and players want to achieve the best results they can in the time allotted. No player wants to be part of a lifeless, dull interpretation of anything, whether there is an audience present or not, as it is not good for the soul! Apparently Mravinsky demanded a minimum of eight rehearsals even if he'd conducted the piece many times before! Good authority says that he was always making new discoveries in the works in question – I trust the end result was worth it and the musicians were still at peace with the world after the performance![4]

We have fewer rehearsals per concert and less recovery time between performances than other nationalities have allocated, and foreign conductors have to accept this. Whilst working on one programme, we are already practising certain passages that are to appear in a forthcoming schedule. Time is of the essence, and there is a great physical strain on our muscles and tendons in order to produce the goods on the night. Once the neck or shoulder muscles are over strained, then it takes time for the inflammation to settle again. By tradition, English orchestras have always kept something in reserve for the concert, and refused to go over the top at the final rehearsal, expecting the conductor to appreciate this fact.

Musicians have grown up from an early age with the idea that they should keep an eye on the clock. (I certainly make sure I have a good view of the one in the studio!) Lesson times have been strictly monitored each week and daily practice at home has had to achieve the maximum results in minimum time. It is a discipline that has been learnt the hard way long before taking any audition. While our contemporaries have been relaxing and enjoying their moments of leisure, the would-be musician has discovered that time is money and the effort needed to improve quickly takes all available concentration. So an orchestra's first collective rehearsal requirement is that precious time is not wasted, and a good conductor is one who is able to achieve the best results in the shortest possible time.

Our orchestra has a few hidden gems up its sleeve, which

---

[4] Jose Antonio Bowen,editor of *The Cambridge Companion to Conducting,* (Cambridge University Press, 2003) 198

can catch out new conductors if they are not forewarned. Certain numbers like 69 and 99 cause some amusement (someone must have read the Kama Sutra in years gone by); 64 always pre-empts a whistle of the tune, 'When I'm 64' as does '76 trombones', but our trademark response has to be the word 'G sharp'! There is a variety of explanations from the older members of the band as to why G sharp should be so special, but it is also surprising that, more often than not, *this* is the note that has to be corrected, especially for the transposing instrumentalists. A strange conductor can be overwhelmed by this reaction, thinking it is something at their expense. This is not necessarily true: it is a way of keeping everyone attentive and produces communal enjoyment. Eventually most conductors catch on to this and either exploit the situation and join in the fun or accept that a completely quiet rehearsal room is a sleepy one.

Going back to the 1960s, one trainee conductor wished to fill in the remaining half hour of a morning rehearsal going through the accompaniment to Elgar's cello concerto, in preparation for the afternoon session. As the orchestra had played this piece regularly there was some annoyance at this suggestion, so much so that all the brass players suddenly decided to swap instruments, to give themselves an extra challenge. All went well until they were asked to repeat a certain passage by themselves which nearly gave the game away!

April 1st jokes have also made their mark. A rehearsal for 'Peter and the Wolf' in preparation for a family concert came to a halt when the whole orchestra had been primed to add an extra beat into one particular bar of Peter's theme somewhere in the middle of the work. Tensions were running high when the opening pages of the piece took longer to rehearse than expected and fears were raised that we would not reach the pin-pointed bar before noon. The bar was reached, the conductor stopped and repeated the passage wondering what on earth had gone wrong, and then the penny slowly dropped to the amusement of all, conductor included. 'Well done, everyone! Now let's try again!' Violinists who constantly have to lean forward on to the edge of their seats to see what markings are going into the part of the desk in front are very susceptible to a 'friend' putting a plastic cup on their seat, hoping it is going to make quite a noise when they sit down again. A distraction at the time, perhaps, but this lightens the mood ready for serious concentration once again.

Naturally, for conductors who bring their own parts, bowed and marked up, this situation would never arise. String players have not spent years trying to improve their technique to find themselves forced to rub out perfectly good and reliable bowings to be substituted often for inferior ones. This is not to say that there is only one way of looking at things. Sometimes changes make a huge improvement to the sound and feel of a passage of music. All desks have to make sure their bowings match and if you've played the same section thirty times before with one particular bowing it is extremely hard to relearn it under pressure. I liken this to being told that for today the word for a 'cat' is a 'dog' and the word for a dog is a 'squirrel'. If the conversation revolved round pets for that day, how confused would you be? Talking of 'squirrels' reminds me of an occasion many years ago when Günther Herbig was our principal guest conductor. He wanted us to perform a ritardando in one particular bar and was interested to know what everyone had suddenly written down in their music. 'It's a squiggle!' someone on the front desk explained. 'A squirrel?' he asked. 'No, a squiggle!' came the reply. Deeper explanations would have interrupted a flowing rehearsal, so we happily continued until the break time, when the translation could be explained further. Ever since that moment, however, we always pass back the message that there is a squirrel over those few bars!

Correcting parts has always seemed like secretarial work. Even though it is quicker when each desk make their own alterations, the process is time consuming and, for those not immediately involved, a chance for the mind to wander far away. Sir Henry Wood was known to spend innumerable hours editing individual orchestral parts, finally autographing them 'Corrected, Henry J.Wood.' With the arrival of computer generated parts, he could have saved himself hours and hours of hard labour probably under very poor lighting conditions. We certainly appreciate it when Günther brings his own bowed copies of Brahms and Bruckner. How refreshing it is to concentrate on the quality of the music with bow in hand rather than a pencil. Changes can still be

10

made but all directions are clearly visible and it is our fault if we are criticised for not following them. Conductors with large repertoires cannot ascribe to this situation, but I do hope they realise that they are starting at a disadvantage.

Variety is the spice of life, we're told, and that certainly applies when the identical orchestral part has to be used for two different conductors and performances.

One conductor might want strong accents on both first and second beats of a bar in 2/4 time, and another demand first beats to be strong and second ones weak. One conductor might tell the orchestra to follow all the printed directions set out in the parts, and the next one could become frustrated if the orchestra does not read between the lines. One might spend too much time on one piece without any feeling of improvement and another might use too little time for players to feel confident in certain passages. Getting a balance between what a conductor wants to rehearse for his own well being and what the players themselves need is therefore quite tricky. Experience must convince more mature minds that a bit of give and take works wonders in the overall scheme of things.

There are certain times when players really need reassuring that they are feeling the right emotions at the right time. If they catch the eye of the conductor, then they have that added confidence to go for it and produce their best, however nervous they might be. Looking away from the music is a risk for the player, because they have to remember where they were on the page in order to regain their place. If this is just before an important solo, the last thing they want to do is falter and destroy the moment for themselves and their colleagues. Hans von Bülow issued the immortal words, 'You must have the score in your head and not your head in the score.'[5] For the conductor's part, he cannot possibly catch everyone's eye at the same moment, but this has to be a trick of his trade, and he must appear to be everything to everyone if he is to achieve that special turn of phrase. Each

---

[5] Peter Loel Boonshaft, *Teaching Music with Passion*, (Meredith Music Publications,2002) 55

11

participant wants to feel that their contribution is adding to the whole, and this personal contact, albeit from a safe distance, is exactly what helps the situation.

Whereas Claudio Abbado would communicate through the hands, eyes and facial expression, [6] Karajan, of course, preferred to conduct with his eyes closed.[7] This just goes to prove that everyone has to find their own way of doing things – fingering difficult passages, counting bars and rests, and communicating with one, two or no eyes at all! Seiji Ozawa has even maintained that the use of the nose cannot be overlooked, because you can smell when the orchestra is about to come adrift and must be prepared to react quickly to get things back on track- just like driving a car on a straight road, when you never know if you're going to have to swerve suddenly to avoid unforeseen danger. [8]

Although the conductor is the medium between composer and player, he is also the focal point for the audience as an actor besides being an inspiration for the players who would really like to play better than they think humanly possible. Bryden Thomson, principal conductor at the time of my joining the BBC Northern Symphony Orchestra, was a fantastic technician. Ask him to conduct seven in one hand and nine with the other and perform an Irish jig all at the same time – I doubt there would have been a problem! He was one of the best accompanists we ever worked with. His conducting of 'The Young Musician of the Year' was exemplary when all musicians on stage jumped a bar with his connivance when the young soloist managed to lose her way for a fraction of a second. Walter Susskind was also a great showman and was so fascinating to watch you could easily forget important entries because you were mesmerised by his antics on the podium. Walter also holds the record for speaking too much. One cold wet morning, sitting in a cramped rehearsal room, we were all tuned up ready for action. Walter emerged in his built up shoes (he was quite short in stature, so had specially-made shoes to give him that extra height). He then started on a detailed explanation of

---

[6] Matheopoulos 74
[7] Jose Antonio Bowen 12
[8] Matheopoulos 394

something probably relating to the Strauss we were about to play but like most musicians, my mind had switched off after the first five minutes, I must confess. Forty minutes later Walter was still talking! Coming to his senses, he went deathly quiet, took a deep breath, and then agreed that it was really time to take a break and get some fresh air! It was an hour later than expected that 'Don Juan' began to emerge from the Milton Hall in Deansgate, Manchester, the cramped headquarters of the BBC Northern at that time.

'A very common problem is giving an upbeat in one tempo and the succeeding downbeat and further beats in another tempo' recalled Günther Schüller in 'The Compleat Conductor'. ' This drives orchestras crazy; and the conductor in question will have totally lost the respect of the musicians after two or three such inept moves, particularly if he fails to realise that the resultant rhythmic shakiness is *his* fault, not the orchestra's.'[9]

Max Rudolph expects the conductor to 'breathe' with the players and almost 'put the notes in their mouths', and Hermann Scherchen even insisted an orchestra should refuse to play if a conductor tried to learn his job from the rostrum!

Orchestras do indeed have great respect for conductors who obviously know the score inside out before the first rehearsal. Vassily Sinaisky, to name but one, seems to know how all conductors in the past have manoeuvred certain phrases and then has made up his own mind on what might work best for us all. He can change opinion from one day to the next and bring out hidden gems in the inner parts that no-one else has ever discovered. This is his forte, his imagination never stops, and you have to respect that he is always striving for more and more from the clues on the pages. (He is well known in the local music shop for searching through the CDs to find even more obscure recordings of different masterpieces.)

Some conductors go to more trouble in marking their scores than others. For those who intend to prepare one score of

---

[9]Günther Schuller, *The Compleat Conductor* (London: Oxford University Press, 1997) 19

the work under study, once and for many years to come, it makes sense to spend time and effort on a multi-coloured chart which often seems to dominate the printed text: blue for the winds, red for the brass, etc. After studying the scores Andre Previn is known to take them to the piano to find out approximately what's going on, even though this eliminates about nine tenths of the music. He then marks the scores with red pencils, blue pencils, black pencils, for structural things like phrase lengths and suggested bowings in erasable pencil. "I have found that if I make a mark on the score it helps to fix it in my mind. The way most of us work nowadays puts an enormous pressure on our time, so I need every short cut I can think of, as we all do too many concerts in a year."[10]

The sight of a score littered with different colours is very comforting to players; it does at least mean that the conductor has taken the time to trouble-shoot and should be able to answer in an informed way any questions that might arise from the rehearsal. On the other hand, there is a danger, or an implication, that you haven't spent enough time really getting to know the notes if you rely too much on your markings. Martyn Brabbins likens this to using a sat-nav rather than a road map. He says he doesn't like to see student's score covered in reds and blues and purples and all the crescendos and diminuendos duly marked. He thinks that it misses the point, and it's unmusical. To treat a contemporary score simply as a series of notes and dynamics and orchestrations is, in his view, as futile as treating Beethoven in that way. He tries to ensure that new pieces are not only accurate, but have some sort of fluidity to them.

Sir Georg Solti said he used to learn scores at the piano but found it was like taking morphine. 'You play and you think it's wonderful, but you realise you don't hear it in your head. You must go through the slow procedure of sitting at a desk and reading the score…first reading the score note by note, bar by bar. I have to be very methodical because if I know that I have 200 pages to learn I will never even start! But if I know I must learn 20 pages a day for ten days then I can do it. After this, I begin to imagine the form of the piece, how it should sound. I read it again

---

[10] Matheopoulos 68,69

and this time I start singing, conducting, making noises, imagining the speed, dynamics. When I feel I know it, only then do I listen to a recording.' 'Conducting styles, like everything else, are affected by fashion. Conducting without a score˙ became fashionable, perhaps, because of Toscanini, whose eyesight was so bad he couldn't read the music on the podium so he managed without it. This gave the false impression that to be a great conductor you have to work without the score.' [11] Stokowski is known to have said that, in his opinion, the ideal way was to conduct with the score, yet know the music from memory![12]

The art of retaining a score lasting over an hour in one's memory is an amazing feat, probably easier for some people to aspire to than others and the fact of having to turn so many pages must necessarily provide quite a distraction to one's thoughts. Even so, there is certainly a feeling among orchestral players that at times conducting is much easier than what is required in actually producing the notes on the page, so mistakes from the podium do not get much of a sympathetic reaction, however demanding the job really is. Of course we all slip up at times, but somehow we expect the conductor, who after all has only the music to consider, to make fewer mistakes than us lesser mortals!

'Musicians also know that, even with very famous and popular conductors, many times *they* save the conductor from serious embarrassment by *not* playing what the maestro conducts. The point is – and all musicians know this, while audiences mostly don't – that a conductor's baton makes no sound, and conductor's mistakes therefore will go unnoticed by the audience (and even most critics, but not by the musicians). But if the musicians were to actually *play* the conductor's mistakes, everyone would hear them.' [13] As Pierre Monteux once told his students: 'When you make a mistake you must admit it, but of course' –he added with a smile – 'you must not make mistakes too often.'

It is very seldom that conductors will give an incorrect cue to a player. Errors are more likely to occur in premieres of works

---

[11] Younghusband 200
[12] Boonshaft 75
[13] Schuller 19

when both the players and the conductor are communally struggling to join two bars together, with beating patterns often changing very quickly one after the other. Computer generated parts might be small and spidery so mistakes can happen quite inadvertently because of the distance involved from the eyes to the printed page. Sir Adrian Boult was once asked what he thought young conductors should concentrate on most of all. 'Not to get in the way' was his wholehearted reply. Most orchestral players would second that!

A lovely analogy of what yielding some control from the podium must feel like is described by Frederik Prausnitz in his book, 'Score and Podium'. He likens the conductor to a fly fisherman trying to hook his trout, and how the angler has to judge when to yield and when to take control again in order to land his catch. How much leeway are you going to allow the musicians in front of you, and are you prepared to take such risks in order to achieve a higher level of performance? Most orchestras would welcome the chance of working with these challenges in mind - to expect the unexpected, and be excited by the unpredictability of it all. Therein lies the genius that we aspired to during many years of hard study!

Seiji Ozawa agreed that conducting was very heavy work. 'If you are physically stiff or tense, then your ears are not really open. The nerves and muscles in your head, all those nerves around the ears must also be relaxed, so that your ears can open up to the sound. And one of the hardest things to learn is how not to close your ears while moving your hands.'[14]

Sir Charles Mackerras reminds us that in German repertory theatres conductors have to tackle different operas all the time with no orchestral or stage rehearsals, as these were limited to new productions only, with a new cast for every performance, and he was tied to beating the score exactly as always practised in that particular house. Did that mean that the conductor couldn't bring any sort of 'interpretation' to the performance? Even under such conditions he said it was amazing how many interpretations one could get because of the unconscious projection of the conductor's

---

[14] Matheopoulos 386

personality, and the effect this had on the players.[15]

James Levine was 'sure that during a performance more mysterious things would happen, because something in the sound, something in the rubato, some of the nuances and subtleties are communicated by one's chemical rapport with the orchestra in the same way that they are in personal relationships. It either happens or it doesn't and sometimes it does and sometimes it doesn't. His philosophy was that we should try to have all the tangible elements as much under control as possible. Only then would there be a better chance of getting the Gods involved and having them smile on us'.[16] Obviously, a conductor cannot take his 'live instrument' home with him, to spend hour after hour practising various techniques until he gets the tone to his satisfaction as would any other professional musician. So how does the young conductor learn to wave his magic wand to control all these magical qualities?

---

[15] Matheopoulos 322
[16] Matheopoulos 284

2nd Mov. : ADAGIO
I want to be a conductor

'Exactly how you conduct, I don't know. It is partly conscious, partly not conscious but the basic issue is simple: you either have a talent to lead or you don't and nobody can teach you that. Watching a young conductor for five minutes you know if he is leading or swimming. The swimmer never makes it, the leader always leads. That's the first criterion'. [17]

An orchestra cannot survive for long without a conductor; a conductor cannot survive at all without players in front of him, interpreting his gestures as best they can. Each individual player expects to be learning his craft for anything up to fifteen years before he can even begin to think about applying to professional orchestras or freelancing in general. One would naturally assume that the gestation period of a conductor would be longer: there is more to learn; more people to influence; more control over the final product; greater publicity for the individual; greater financial rewards for the successful; greater strain on the emotions, mind and body. Make one mistake, one false move, and thousands of people could be watching and suffering the consequences. Who would want to put themselves to this sort of exposure?

Spending time in Europe was advocated by Lorin Maazel as it gave the opportunity to absorb many kinds of idiomatic playing, the knowledge of several languages and of the cultural differences of many places. Sir Adrian Boult had extraordinary advice for wannabe conductors and that was to think about getting another job! 'Only embark on a career if you feel that you'd rather put your head in a gas oven if you couldn't conduct.' [18]

The traditional ways of learning the basic techniques involve post graduate study in Britain and abroad. The course at the Royal Academy in London takes three years with emphasis on the laws of cause and effect to enable students to convey convincingly and unambiguously their musical intentions to the

---

[17] Younghusband 189
[18] Matheopoulos 144

orchestra. Manchester maintains a two year course which is very intensive, and that of the Royal Scottish Academy is a year less. All try to give students as many opportunities to conduct as possible, watch rehearsals of the local professional orchestras, and invite recognised conductors to demonstrate their particular skill. Russia was dominated by the teaching of Ilya Musin in St.Petersburg until his death in 1999. Anyone who did not stay for the whole five year course left without a qualification. His maxim was that you must make music visible with your hands, and that you used the baton as artists would use the tip of their paintbrush. Finland glories in the art of Jorma Panula who has been responsible for many young maestros at the Sibelius Academy in Helsinki. He has been called 'the maestro of the maestros' and he insisted that the conductors at the academy should have the opportunity to work with an orchestra as the Russians do and not a pianist. He advocated conducting ballet as a medium that had to concentrate the mind on both the activities of the orchestra and the performers on stage. Many of his conversations and discussions would take place within the confines of the sauna - a typically Finnish occupation!

Training in Germany involved practical knowledge of at least one instrument from each of the different sections of the orchestra, alongside studies of psychology, philosophy, counterpoint, and music theory. Again this would take five years and one needed a pass in the final exam to qualify. No qualification meant no employment.

Austria had Hans Swarowsky, a pupil of Schonberg, who emphasised the importance of projecting the characteristic style of the music and advocated the idea of achieving maximum musical communication with the most economical means. He often had a student conduct with one hand while playing from a piano reduction of the orchestra score with the other. Italians, on the other hand, depended on Franco Ferrara for their inspiration. Although he himself conducted only a few bars at a time, his demonstrations showed that he could communicate with special intensity. After five minutes' explanation, everything was apparently crystal clear.

America doesn't appear to have a standard conducting

course. Different universities have come up with really good ideas at different times, but when the funding has gone the courses disappear in a cloud. What they do have is a number of summer courses like that at Tanglewood, which have been immensely popular. Lorin Maazel ran a conductors' symposium at Cleveland for a number of years where applicants were asked to write down a page of a prescribed score from memory. If they achieved this they were allowed to rehearse the orchestra for eight minutes, performing the piece straightaway. Sir Georg Solti held some master classes in Chicago for which two hundred applicants were finally reduced to a mere half dozen.

An alternative route into the profession is the hype of conducting prizes and competitions. The Koussevitzky prize awarded every summer at Tanglewood was given to Claudio Abbado in 1958; five years later he won the first Dmitri Mitropoulos competition, which offered a cash prize and a season's engagement as an assistant to Leonard Bernstein at the New York Philharmonic. The panel of the Karajan conductors' competition looked for someone with a compulsive and penetrating temperament rather than a proficient conductor-someone having enough conviction to impress the orchestra as well as the audience. The girl friend of Seiji Ozawa persuaded him to enter the Besançon competition, where he won first prize, enabling him to join Karajan's conducting classes in Berlin for eight months. Riccardo Muti won the prize at the Guido conductors' competition in 1967, which gave him an opening to Philadelphia and Eugene Ormandy. Simon Rattle benefited from two years as assistant conductor of the Bournemouth Symphony and its Sinfonietta after winning first prize in the John Player competition. George Hurst has provided a fatherly, caring role there for young conductors, and the players themselves would also give some feed-back and friendly advice. Vernon Handley, always known as Tod, had problems when he was young as he didn't play an instrument. He used the scores to learn the works, hence his study of way out things by Bax, Rubbra, Ireland etc. He would demonstrate to students how you could use the baton to produce certain effects – great to have a few tricks up your sleeve.

Although not advertised as a full scale competition, the

BBC Philharmonic was asked to take part in a workshop, designed specifically to assist would-be-conductors in their training period. This was to take place over a week, with guidance from Yan Pascal Tortelier and Martyn Brabbins and culminating in a final televised performance at the Bridgewater Hall, Manchester, with three of the conductors chosen as having the greatest potential at that time. The finalist out of these three would have the opportunity of more help and guidance during the following year, with the possibility of conducting the Philharmonic on future occasions, either for certain pieces or whole programmes. This was a follow-on event from a series called 'Young Musician of the Year' which had attracted large audience figures, providing plenty of interest from the general public.

The underlying idea of this event was obviously a bonus for any aspiring conductor, as opportunities to work with professional orchestras are so very few and far between. The age limit was 26, so a certain number of entrants were still undergraduates. All had been well educated, and had already conducted performances ranging from Mozart to Shostakovich and Bartok. All were asked to explain why they had put their names forward in the first place.

- "The workshop provides a unique opportunity to work with a professional orchestra, a privilege that is at present virtually non-existent to young conductors like me. I would be fascinated to work with the two workshop leaders, to learn from their vast experience, and to be able to get some feedback from world class players and tutors with regard to technique and interpretation is of paramount importance to me. Conducting is a continual learning process; any experience is valuable be it with a youth group, amateur ensemble or semi-professional orchestra but for a determined conductor who has faith in himself and his abilities, this opportunity would seem to be a perfect next step in my continuing musical education."

- "I want to test my ability to conduct and learn from a great orchestra. This means offering musical leadership and demonstrating the power to interpret music and communicate it

21

at the highest level. A participant of the workshop and potential assistant conductor requires leadership, responsibility and the desire to learn from the insight and experience of leading professional conductors, respected orchestral musicians and administrators. I wish to take up the challenge."

- "The workshop would provide me with a situation which is not available in the normal course of study at a conservatory, or in a rehearsal for which the young conductor is entirely responsible. I would be able to learn in a professional situation about the practicalities of dealing with an orchestra. As an assistant conductor one can learn about the daily running of an orchestra and see how an experienced conductor deals with professional players in a practical work situation – with all the problems of working within a busy schedule to produce concerts of the highest standard, as well as gaining invaluable experience in working with the orchestra. The Philharmonic has an exciting mix of standard and more adventurous repertoire, employing the best of international conductors. The assistantship would be the opportunity of a life-time for a young conductor."

- "Until recently, I believe there has been an element missing from the training of young British conductors - opportunity. I now need to work with an ensemble which is concerned with the music expression, rather than technical facility, as well as gaining access to music that is less practical for a semi-professional orchestra. The workshop will provide invaluable feedback from a whole range of musicians on one's own conducting and, hopefully, some helpful advice."

- "Very few conductors have the chance to gain experience with professionals. The constructive atmosphere of such a workshop, as opposed to the pressure of a competition, offers insight and experience of a kind that cannot be gained within a music college. To be given the chance to make music and to discuss technique and interpretation with some of its members is an extremely exciting prospect. Since a conductor learns from his mistakes and it is the players who have to respond to what he is doing, the critical feedback is immensely helpful."

The week progressed with rehearsals of Debussy's 'La Mer', Britten's 'Young Person's Guide to the Orchestra', and extracts from Beethoven's Symphony No.2. All members of the orchestra were invited to give marks out of ten for each conductor, giving suggestions and reasons for their decision. When the results were collated, the average score was low, with many players being tempted to award minus numbers! Here are some of the comments, for and against, finishing with off the cuff remarks made to the camera during the filming of the production.

- *Good natural direction and flow in the music and phrasing – gave structure to the pieces and knew the score; nice manner. He conveys the music within his beat, not just the notes and dynamics.*

Once the music has started together players need more than a time beater to uplift the performance away from something a computer could churn out. All musicians need to feel the peaks and troughs of phrases, breathe, be persuaded to enjoy similar emotions, be they joyous, fearful or threatening. Only when we work as one does the music become alive to the players and finally the audience. It may be true that we need to be cajoled into this some of the time, but it helps if the conductor has gained our respect and trust, so we have something clear to follow and we are free to work on our production of the sounds to make a coherent whole. A pleasant manner is generally all that is required to achieve this – no-one in the room has spent years and years of training and discipline to sit in a section and not be totally involved in the proceedings.

- *Able to adapt to different styles; good speaking manner – not arrogant!*

According to Harold Farberman in his essay on training conductors, he makes the point that 'the increasing virtuosity of the orchestra has made the job of the modern conductor easier; modern professionals are capable of playing much standard repertoire without any leadership at all.'[19]   We expect the conductor to know the score very much better than we do, bearing in mind that many of the players will have performed the work in question many more times than the novice conductor. However, as no two performances will ever be exactly the same, even on successive days, rehearsal time is there for the conductor to impress his personality and interpretation of the score on his colleagues. He has the final say, after all.

So, when addressing the orchestra, it is important for him to get everyone involved, not just the front few desks of string players. The warmth and vitality of sound will come if all the string players feel they have an important role to play. We're all totally dependant on each other. Peter Boonshaft warns us that players who are not engaged in rehearsals will 'use every quarter-note rest to look at the clock in frustration'. He suggests that a soft mumble audible to the first row is not a good idea, but a few well-chosen words, enunciated clearly and succinctly will indeed get results. A change of pace, volume and voice inflection would also keep the interest and provide a more enjoyable rehearsal.[20] It goes without saying that politeness is the key; we're all human beings striving towards the same goal.

- *Did some proper balancing, and made intelligent comments from what he had heard.*

Student conductors might well practise in front of a mirror or along with their iplayer, but in the real world they have to be able to react to what is going on in front of them. If the ensemble is not together, it is so frustrating for the players, and it should be the conductor who sorts it out. Sometimes there are wrong notes on the printed page; if the players can hear them, they expect the conductor to as well. When rehearsals are not going terribly well, a musician with a transposing instrument might stop proceedings to query a few notes (which might or might not be in his copy – I'm never absolutely sure!). Conductors who know the score so well in advance have no problem with this. In fact knowing the score

---

[19] Bowen 249
[20] Boonshaft 119

inside out must surely make it easier to concentrate on the sound that the orchestra is producing at present.

- *Was aware of tempo changes before they happened. Nice feel for upbeats; quick in noticing directions to give us, like dynamics.*

It has been said often that orchestras can perform well without a conductor.

Sir Thomas Beecham declared: 'There are two golden rules for an orchestra – start together and finish together. The public doesn't give a damn what goes on in between!' However, players need help before tempo changes so that everyone can change gear together. Anticipation of the new tempo too early destroys the moment of surprise for the listener and reaction too late, with head buried in the score, is no good either. It is multi-tasking, like steering a car and talking on a mobile phone. Both are dangerous occupations, only one is legal! Peter Boonshaft describes his two simple rules:1) give the players something meaningful to watch - cues, facial expressions or gestures - that mean something to them; and 2) give them something meaningful to hear – that is, inspire them, give them corrections that truly make things better, and give them enormous amounts of positive reinforcement.[21]

- *Clear and decisive; real presence and authority.*

'A prepared conductor would already know where problems are likely to be and what was needed to fix them. That is efficiency! That saves time! When the conductor really knows his score he can rapidly move from measure to measure correcting problems, offering abundant cues and executing gestures with surgical precision.'[22] I can remember Solti directing us in a very uplifting performance of the 'Four last Songs' of Strauss with Dame Kiri te Kawana in the mid- 70s. What warmth he was able to achieve from the strings! 'Don't take any notice of the 'p' at the opening of the final movement.' he said. 'Now play it again much softer but *think* of the forte sound you have just made.'

---

[21] Boonshaft 111-2
[22] Boonshaft 69

- *Looked at the instrumentalists who were playing and did not have his head in the score.*

Eye contact is everything to an orchestral player. In Max Rudolph's book he recommends that eyes are an invaluable means of establishing personal contact between the conductor and the players. Therefore, they should be used as much as possible, with the minimum amount of time spent in looking at the score. If you cannot entirely memorize the music, you must still be able to keep your attention on the orchestra most of the time, referring to the score only at intervals of several bars. With training you could learn to see a number of bars at once, so that by glancing down you would not lose your place in the score. Max maintains that it is not only the preparatory gesture but the way you look at a player that can tell him in advance what kind of expression is expected of him.

- *Commanding voice; doesn't just play through the piece unnecessarily.*

Even 70 years ago orchestras hated rehearsing for rehearsing sake. Only when this was vitally necessary would they be willing to go over passages or movements again and again. Toscanini would work on a few selected passages, but was never known to insist on playing the whole movement through just for its' own sake.

- *Seemed to realise he needed the orchestra on his side.*

Players soon realise if they are only rehearsing for the conductor's sake, and this is fatal for an effective collaboration.

- *Perhaps should try a little less hard.*

Audiences do not want to know how difficult certain pieces might be to perform; they buy their tickets in order to be taken out of themselves, entertained and transported to a more heavenly place. They can admire the concentration levels on stage, but would become uneasy if they became aware of a player's panic and anguish. The same could be said about the relationship of player/conductor. Players need the reassurance that the conductor knows what he is doing. A lack of confidence on the podium can spread through an orchestra very quickly, affecting their own concentration levels and causing unwanted mistakes. We all want a performance to be enjoyable and need all the help we can get! Players seemed to concentrate on two critical points: problems with baton technique and lack of personality.

1. Can't keep tempo going; too many mannerisms that get in the way.
2. An expressive beat that has no control over the orchestra.
3. Doesn't give music time to breathe.
4. No distinction given to three beats in a bar; looks like two from the side.
5. Strange beat that looks like a snake.
6. Conducts the ceiling and wobbles around all over the place.
7. Some bars do not seem to be equal in length - some beats early, some late.
8. All the nuances in the score seem to be missing from the beat.
9. Seemed to react to all the dynamics rather than anticipating them.
10. Ignores the musicians who have difficult passages to play.
11. Music appears to be an intellectual exercise; when they realise there is a tune being played, the tempo slows down.
12. No energy or showbiz, making performance bland and pointless.
13. Ungainly, irritating, patronising; dull, vague, tepid.
14. A confident manner verging on the irritating.
15. Much more eye contact would improve matters, especially for wind soloists.
16. Unaware there is an orchestra in front - perhaps more used to a CD.
17. Facial expression says 'I'm scared!' not 'This is how I feel about the music.'
18. Doesn't seem to realise that the orchestra know the piece very well and are waiting to be told more than basic points.
19. Trying too hard to look good.
20. Would benefit from ten years' experience as an orchestral player, as he would then know what is required and expected.

And finally, opinions from the players interviewed in front of the cameras were mysteriously of a more polite nature:

Violinist: I think they are being quite brave.

Violinist: A lot of members find it hard enough when a 'normal' conductor comes along. There's a fine line between having authority and creating chaos.

Cellist: It's very easy for someone to come along and beat time; the net result is what the orchestra would have played anyway.

Clarinettist: It's always been a complete mystery to me why someone should want to stand and do something silent. I have never understood this - they must be ego-maniacs!

Bassoonist: I was a bit disappointed by the standard, to be frank, but I think it is a fantastic pressure on them.

Percussionist: A clear beat obviously, but there has to be musicality behind that.

Percussionist: We're looking for someone with real knowledge of the music, real insight into how it will go, and have ideas on interpretation.

Trumpeter: All we need is a good upbeat…. and we'll be OK!

Orchestral players are well known to be suspicious of untried talent on the podium for all the reasons given above. After such a full and stressful week for the applicants, did they themselves consider it a worthwhile venture in retrospect? Would they put themselves through such a trauma again if the situation arose? Could they recommend the experience to anyone else? What could they take away with them to help them in their quest for the Holy Grail? Here are some of their reminiscences:

- "Few students on conducting courses in this country are British; out of six on my course, I was the only one for a while. Music colleges here are still struggling to justify the existence of a conducting course. In Russia you might start on such a course when you are in the mid- twenties and still be there five years later. I looked for a course that had trained people who were now earning their living from conducting. There are a number of competitions abroad but very few in Britain. Also, few orchestras can afford to have associate conducting posts, so one has to audition for every single job or competition that comes up and hope to get that lucky foot in the door. Working with amateur groups doesn't help much because coming here is a completely different kettle of fish. Professionals do not need to be pushed or held back - you need to trust them far more. That is one of the main things that I have learned this week."

- "I found it enormously useful and stressful. No-one in a competition would ask you to try something out in a different way, which puts you on the spot. Taking over the rehearsal in short bursts wasn't easy as adrenalin levels were difficult to control. Had all rehearsals been on video then you could have replayed them at a later date and taken more from them. You could then see quite clearly why you were interrupted at a certain point. However, it is rare that you work together with other conductors."

- "I'm disappointed that there is no apparent funding in place for another event like this one. If you can nurture the young conductors early on and show them how they can get the right sort of responses from an orchestra, then this is extremely valuable. Also, getting to know the musicians you are working with is a bonus, and if you could just find the right gesture, and the right way of getting the orchestra on your side, then what a wonderful experience that would be! The most rewarding part of the job is to get the respect of the musicians and have the knowledge that they have enjoyed working with you."

- "With conducting, your ultimate instrument is a top grade orchestra that you've probably never ever conducted before. So it is like learning the violin, but not ever actually playing it! The workshop highlighted the fact that there were things that you thought you needed to show that were unnecessary, whereas on a deeper level, things that players really wanted, you were sadly lacking in providing. It was then a problem returning to the student orchestral situation and having to show the beats and omit all the finer details."

- "The workshop was like a benchmark and gave me an idea of what sort of things were lacking from my training so far. Conducting in front of two pianos gave experience, but nothing could prepare you for the shock of controlling a large orchestra. Experience is what is needed, and the confidence will follow gradually."

- "It was just a great experience all round really, and people assume now that I know what I'm doing, having taken part in the workshop and performed on TV. I can say I've conducted a professional orchestra which is something that many people can only dream about and never achieve. That is a very positive thing to take away with me."

The actual training of a conductor was quite a late phenomenon. In fact, the first treatise to appear on conducting was probably the 12 pages written by Berlioz in 1855; and Vincent d'Indy started a course in Paris in1905.The first course in England was set up by Sir Adrian Boult at the Royal College of Music in 1919. He was overheard to say 'There is very little chance of making a living out of conducting, but there is every chance for most people to get a great deal of pleasure out of it in their spare time.'[23] Yet it was 1950 before Max Rudolph attempted to add expression to conducting, offering one page at the end of his treatise to describe how the direction of a beat could be changed for a particular result. In fact basic beat patterns have changed little over the years, bringing us to the conclusion (as Harold Farberman says) that we continue to graduate nineteenth-century conductors in the twenty-first century. He advocates the need for fresh ideas, open minds, and a willingness to create a rapport with a new technical proficiency based on the demands of the music. [24]

At the very least, the idea of enjoying oneself is paramount for the survival of all performers and audience alike! So are orchestras right to expect the very highest level of director or is that a dream world where time and money are abundant?

How easily could we change the attitude of orchestras to meet the trainees half way? Should the conservatoires be expected to offer a wider curriculum to fill up the shortfalls in the present systems?

---

[23] Adrian C. Boult, *A Handbook on the Technique of Conducting,* (Hall the Printer Ltd. Oxford) 3

[24] Bowen 249

Would similar workshops really offer sufficient help to satisfy the hunger of the conductors who are desperate to improve with the right sort of practice time and the musicians at the receiving end? Perhaps there are other ways of highlighting a growing problem or, indeed, bringing the whole arena of music more to the attention of the general public.

Classical concerts rarely get an airing on TV as they are described as having minority appeal. Take away the BBC Proms in the summer and the remaining schedules have only a handful of programmes with classical connections. So imagine the surprise to find a series entitled 'Maestro' shown over a number of weeks on BBC 2. This was a series of programmes to instruct eight celebrities to the extent that they could control a performance given by the BBC Concert Orchestra. There were actors, news presenters, and pop musicians, some who could play an instrument and some who could not even read music. The panel of judges consisted of well known maestros and the final vote from the orchestral players was used to whittle down the number of contenders each week, leaving only one the opportunity of conducting something special in front of thousands of people in Hyde Park, London for the 'Proms in the Park'. There were excerpts shown from the week of training, with each contender having their own mentor (well established conductors in their own right), their initial introduction to the orchestra, and their progress, all documented as the weeks went by. The whole scenario became quite riveting – nobody could guess who was going to win, but the journey there was fascinating

As novel as the idea was initially, it brought to light many myths that conducting appears to be easy as far as the general public are concerned. Although the training sessions that the mentors gave were not seen in full, one could appreciate the results of the training as the orchestra struggled to follow the baton. What a successful series it was for showing how confusing certain mannerisms can be when interpreted by individual players.

Deborah Orr, from The Independent stated,

'It was quite a revelation, seeing just how appalling a noise an untutored conductor could achieve from a group of fine professionals. One had nothing but admiration for the orchestra, who did as they were told, even when being told by an idiot. They no doubt could have played these pieces of music blindfold– Bizet's 'Carmen', Prokofiev's 'Dance of the Knights', Strauss 'Blue Danube', and Grieg's 'In the hall of the Mountain King'. But the illustration of their obedience to even the most inept of direction confirmed that the eight entertainers had all taken on a daunting task. Because it was made so very clear that the eight had wandered into a realm of awesome complexity and skill, the show quickly established itself as weirdly compelling.'[25]

Jason Lai, who was the mentor of the eventual winner of this series, had himself taken part in numerous competitions: winner of the BBC young conductors' workshop in 2002, a finalist in the BBC young composer award 1994, and a prize winner at the Leeds conducting competition in 2005. He was on the panel of 'The Young Musician of the Year' competition in 2006, and was a judge in the BBC classical talent show 'Classical Star' 2007. He was assistant conductor with our orchestra for three years, so I was interested to know how much he thought he had gained from this apprenticeship; how frightening were these competitions? Was it worse being on the panel or taking part as a competitor?

'I think for any young conductor the chance of becoming the assistant conductor to such a big orchestra is a wonderful opportunity and I was thrilled to win the BBC young conductors' workshop and become the assistant to the BBC Phil. But even though that week of workshops running up to the final was really challenging, both nerve-racking and exhilarating, and one of the toughest weeks of my life, I would say winning was the easy part. What came after was the shock. Don't get me wrong - winning the competition was very hard and not something I expected would happen - but what came next... now that WAS hard.

I knew becoming a conductor was always going to be hard but I still remember standing on that podium in front of the Philharmonic for the first time after winning the competition and being absolutely terrified. No one, but no one, can prepare you for that first time in front of a pro band. It doesn't matter what you're

[25] *The Independent, 22/08/08* www.bbc.co.uk/musictv/maestro/news/what-the-papers-said

conducting teachers tell you, when you're up there you are alone, you and the orchestra. I had been asked by the general manager to run through some contemporary pieces written by young composers, so in my mind at least I was just going to be judged on my clarity and not, thank God, what I could do with Beethoven.

It started off well and I looked serious but still quaking inside, and then came what to me was an ice-breaker, something that helped calm me. As I was conducting away I managed to turn two pages by mistake and so I was waving my arms in a completely different number of beats from what the musicians had in front of them. There was a tiny uproar in the orchestra followed by more dissent, so I stopped. The accusations started to come "erm...there are four beats in that bar not seven" "What are you beating there?" "What are you doing?" I looked down at the score and for those agonising few moments I did not know what had happened, my brain was burning, and then I realised. I announced to the orchestra confidently "Sorry but I turned two pages by mistake...Ooops! ..." there was some laughter and a bit of jeering, but after that I felt much better.

I think orchestras sometimes underestimate how hard it is to stand up there, and I know conductors are not the most popular musicians in the world, but the best conductors in my mind manage to direct and also manage to be human and not some ego-ridden maniac who demands complete obedience. The BBC Phil is actually one of the friendliest and most cooperative orchestras I've ever worked with and my time with them, I feel, was great. I learned a lot from them and although there were a few uncomfortable learning curves I felt, after three years with them, I had the tools to become a better conductor. I didn't leave them as the next Simon Rattle, but I did leave them with the knowledge in my mind that I could now become a professional conductor.

Being in front of the camera has never really fazed me, maybe I'm a frustrated actor or TV presenter but even during the workshop week when we were followed by cameras wherever we went, I didn't feel bothered by them. So when I was asked to do some TV work I was up for the challenge. I was chosen to be on the panel for the BBC2 classical talent show 'Classical Star' which aired in 2007. Initially, I was only booked to be a panellist for the first round regional judging but I must have made an impression as I was asked back to be a judge on the televised rounds as well. How the tables had turned and now judging rather than being judged was a strange feeling for me, but as my dreams were fulfilled by winning a competition, it seemed right to offer that chance back to a deserving musician. In truth, I was a little nervous to begin with but soon settled into the role I was asked to fill; in fact, by the end, I loved it.

The TV work just happened, it has never been expected or planned, but my mission in life is to get the message out there that classical music is for everyone and not just for the select few. If I can get this message across in my TV work then that is my goal. Being a conductor already has certain connotations in people's minds of a certain grandeur, a mystique, an unusual job that few people know about or understand (orchestral musicians probably feel the opposite way and I am sure they have less grand names to throw at us!). So, when I was asked to participate in 'Maestro' I was interested but very hesitant.

I figured that teaching a bunch of celebrities would turn the craft of conducting into a joke, but then I had a real think and understood it as a golden opportunity to show what we do and how hard it all is. If it opened up the world of classical music to a new audience then it would be a good thing; so I accepted. I would like to think 'Maestro' televisually was a huge success and winning it with Sue Perkins was just fantastic. It was completely exhausting to do as we had to teach complete novices in a few months what we had learned in many years, and as Sue progressed further and further along I started to get extremely nervous for her.

The TV work continued with a new show for Childrens' BBC called 'Clash' and presenting for 'The Culture Show' and making my conducting debut with the English Chamber Orchestra before returning to Taipei and Bremen to work with orchestras there.

Having a career in music was something I had always wanted but I didn't expect it to turn out as it has done. I've managed to balance my work as a conductor and broadcaster and feel immensely privileged for all the opportunities that have come my way. Malcolm Gladwell in his book 'Outliers' proposes that people who have achieved success in a certain field have worked hard but more importantly been given golden opportunities at certain points in their life. I feel very lucky to have won the BBC conductors' workshop and worked alongside the BBC Phil and it is this that has really put me on this road that I now travel.'

This wasn't the first time that producers had tried to popularise the mysterious world of classical music. Zubin Mehta gave a master class on TV with the Israel Phil. playing Stravinsky's 'Rite of Spring', particularly the 5/4 rhythm which works well as 3 + 2. One student reckoned he could see a rhythm of 2+3 so Mehta let him try it out on the orchestra. Of course it worked well and the young man was delighted. 'Now let the Phil. play it on its own!', and naturally this worked very well too!

Nicholas Kraemer reminded me of another series on television called 'Fake It!' An amateur would receive an intense period of instruction before going into competition with serious advocates of a particular profession. Nicolas was the tutor for the programme involving conductor training which he mentions during his interview later in this book. There was also a series called 'Orchestra' which had appeared on Channel 4 TV in the early 90s, focusing on the workings of the Schleswig Holstein Festival Orchestra, with Sir Georg Solti and the pianist/comedian, Dudley Moore. Sir Georg is quoted as saying how he didn't find conducting technically difficult because he had learnt it over the years, but the most difficult thing was not to be totally satisfied with a performance. You always had to develop, and try harder when you did a piece again. He dreaded the day he could say 'It was very good yesterday,' because that would be the end.'

During the programme, Solti gave Dudley Moore some advice on conducting 'Don Juan' for the first time:

1) The first ingredient you need to be a conductor is to be a maniac about it. You must really believe in what you are doing. You cannot conduct if you have inhibitions.

2) You must have an ability to plunge yourself into the music, especially with a score like 'Don Juan', which is extremely passionate.

3) Before you start, close your eyes and imagine the tempo in

your mind. Keep still, don't move your hands or arms, or you will confuse the musicians.

4) A good upbeat is all it takes, but you must always keep the tempo in mind. When you are beating in two, the one is the luxury, the two is the business.

5) You can beat with your fingers, wrist, your eyes, foot, it really doesn't matter, as long as you have imagination and know what you want.

6) Don't expect miracles. There are no short cuts. I have fought for 45 years to get the down beat and up beat right at the beginning of 'Don Juan'. The metronome is one of the conductor's closest friends. The speed must be right. Too slow it will sound stodgy, too fast and some of the parts will be unplayable.

8) Control the tempo. Holding the speed is very important. You must have a clock inside you – in your body.

9) You must know the music inside out otherwise your head will be buried in the score and that's no good.

10) If you are working with an orchestra you don't know the first thing you must do is look around and ask who is playing first, where they are sitting. You must know where everyone is sitting.

11) Remember that we are working in a large studio and the orchestra is very spread out. By the time the sound reaches you from the back it is already late. You must get them to play on the beat so they don't drag behind.

12) Know when to watch and when to listen. Be 'in' and 'out' of the music.

13) When things aren't working out you must know how to diagnose what is wrong. And say how to correct it. One small thing going wrong can throw the whole orchestra. You must try to understand how the musician's mind works and how each instrument will respond to the person who's trying to make certain technical demands on it.

14) The orchestra/conductor relationship is like the lion and the tamer. As long as the tamer is firm, the lion doesn't eat him up. I prefer to be thought of as a respected friend.

15) Preparation is everything. If you have prepared everything

and rehearsed properly, you should be able to enjoy the concert because the work is done.[26]

---

[26] Younghusband 204,206,208

3rd Mov. : SCHERZO CAPRICCIOSO
The excitement of orchestral life

Solti's analogy of 'lion and tamer' does inspire me to think of the running of an orchestra being similar to a well controlled zoo! We are not kept behind bars or separated into cages, but once the 'tamer' has entered the arena then no one can escape until officially dismissed. All the 'animals' have their own individual characteristics even though we are categorised into sections. Each section has its own leader who is designated to control its pack; each member of the pack has to follow and obey whatever instructions might be given. The supervisors in the zoo get to know the characteristics of their 'pets' as they are interacting with them day in and day out. This relationship works so well that any dissent or upset is picked up almost immediately and steps can be taken quickly to rectify any troublesome situation. I imagine this rapport must take time to build, and any stranger entering the pens would be treated very warily. It is at this stage that the analogy with the players begins to break down. The chief conductor does not experience the same conditions as the players: he hands the baton over to others for weeks at a time and has no control over what they might do to the orchestra in his absence. Even when he does appear, he is separate from the group as he has the use of his own green room at interval time, well away from the players, and often travels separately to concert venues, both here and abroad. It is unlikely that conductors will appear in the same city at the same time. Yan Pascal Tortelier explained to me once that he only met Günther Herbig many years ago because Günther was conducting when Pascal was on the circuit performing violin concertos. So the majority of players have to pool together; they cannot retreat in the same way, and therefore find themselves in a bonding situation like a large family, solving each other's problems and generally looking after one another. This state of affairs is most noticeable when the orchestra is away from home, especially when touring a foreign country. Jessica Harris, a violinist, who had only joined the Phil for a few weeks before being thrown into a tour said: 'Touring is a wonderful opportunity for bonding. The camaraderie is vital.

Living with your fellow-players breaks down barriers, and is a tremendous way to get to know people.'

When an audience see orchestral players assemble on the platform they must have the impression that a serious group of performers is going to entertain them, especially when you consider that the acceptable dress code is sombre but smart looking black evening gowns for the ladies and tails for the gentlemen. Therein belies a tradition that has been passed on from one generation to another and is a hard convention to change. Perhaps what is not so obvious to an observer is that underneath this harsh exterior lie many hidden talents that players might specialise in away from the glare of the platform. Even in Bernard Shore's day an orchestra was a thriving cottage industry and one would be amazed to discover that there is an expert in almost anything you could think of, eager to help his/her colleagues surmount any sort of problem.

Talking to members of our own band, especially during long coach journeys, would reveal many hidden talents and unusual interests: DIY experts who have built staircases in farmhouses, fitted loft ladders up to attics, designed gardens, laid floor tiles, attended to plumbing problems, built and mended computers and studied for Open University degrees. We have some first rate photographers and even an expert juggler and unicyclist!

In previous years, we have had a bassoonist who trained to be a commercial pilot, and who now trains others; a cellist who is now the director of Chetham's Music School in Manchester; a violinist who has become a world expert on Egyptology, producing a beautifully presented book on the subject, with help from one of our photographers and one of our computer experts who designed all the hieroglyphs in a computerised form. Andrew Scrivener, a very popular violinist, had a great spirit of adventure as well as a great pride in belonging to this orchestra. He would explore many exotic places in the holidays, and at one time became intrigued with the music academy at the Old Customs House in Stone Town, Zanzibar where they are trying to foster a local interest in traditional music with lessons in oud, qanun, violin and tabla. After the shock of his sudden death whilst on a climbing holiday in Colombia in 2005 a very moving funeral service was held, attended by almost the whole orchestra with colleagues playing a movement from a Schubert Quintet, and a memorial fund was set up in his name to offer outstanding students in Zanzibar some financial help.

Another violinist became a fitness instructor and took part in the 2000 triathlon world championships in Perth, Australia, and indeed many present members take part in marathons for charity, sponsored generously by their colleagues.

On a musical front, we have recording engineers who produce CDs for brass bands, church choirs and school choirs, and enthusiasts who give demonstrations on Alpenhorns, accordions, and jazz groups, along with players who have arranged music for the Blue Peter programmes and educational work. One or two players are expert at passing round their cartoons with appropriate captions that can cheer up everyone during a rather intense rehearsal.

Another aspect of orchestral life in Manchester has been the formation of a 'Not the Philharmonic Orchestra!'- a brainwave that was initiated as a way of raising money for a handicapped colleague. All members and freelance players are invited to take part, the only catch being that they have to leave their own instrument at home and play something completely different, ideally in a different section! So woodwind players become string players for the day, and string players join the brass section etc. With assistance from the experts, it is amazing how quickly some people become proficient, and rehearsals finally take place near to the concert date. The first performance consisted of the majority of 'The Planets' by Holst, with Britten's 'Young Person's Guide to the Orchestra' coming later and even a version of Stravinsky's 'Wrong of Spring'. Generally the rhythmic features are very tight, although pitch is something else! Often a solo is drowned out by another instrumentalist who cannot play any softer, and it is possible that the whole performance can break down due to fits of laughter or cheers if a passage has gone unexpected well. Dress code is very adventurous with brown bears playing the timps, and some cross dressing going on elsewhere and many players hiding under a variety of wigs. The invited audience all take it in good part: half the fun is guessing who on earth lies underneath the disguise. The whole performance is recorded, warts and all, and contributions are duly accepted when the CD has been formatted. This sort of epic occasion can occur once every ten years or so, but is great for melding the orchestra into an even tighter community. How soothing it is to turn up for work the following day and hear a well tuned chord once again!

After the success of such unusual performances, it did not take long for someone to envisage a special version of Ravel's 'Bolero' for a Blue Peter Prom at the Albert Hall, London. The piece duly started with one cellist and side drum on stage and many empty chairs. As long as players arrived at their desk in time for their musical cue, they were allowed to appear from any direction causing whatever chaos was necessary. Some strolled on chatting, some forgot their instruments and had to run off again, one appeared from inside a double bass case, another with fishing rod in hand. One player had to be removed from the leader's seat and another received a red card for 'bad' behaviour. Imagination ran riot and Yan Pascal Tortelier had no idea what anyone would get up to. Needless to say that the whole episode went down very well with the audience as well as the orchestra, and the management's trust was not in vain.

The idea of learning to play different instruments has inspired me to have a go not only at orchestral mandolin, but also the piano accordion. This has a surprising variety of styles of playing, and has given me many opportunities, including a chance to take part in a televised concert with Luciano Pavarotti; Tchaikovsky's Suite with a group of four accordionists taken out of our string sections; performing as a duo with my violinist husband on a BAC 111 jet on Feb 29th booked to serenade the ladies who were proposing to their fiancés in the skies above Gretna Green one icy evening; and even playing round the tables as part of the entertainment for one of Sir Alex Ferguson's birthday parties! There are people all over the world who hold Manchester United close to their hearts and are always ready to talk about the team players when they realise we come from the same city, so we happily recall this episode with great fondness. Other unusual requests have included learning a concertina specially for a solo in 'Swinton Jig' by Sir Peter Maxwell Davies, and even rewriting a zither part which appears in a score of the 2nd Orchestral Suite of Charles Ives. Why he wrote the open strings two octaves out I shall probably never know!

So, there are strong social bonds for the players that a visiting conductor has little chance of discovering in great detail. This extra perception builds up naturally among the players and is probably why conductors can feel like an outsider. They can be on friendly terms with many players but there is always this reserve - an invisible barrier, large or small, which must be dealt with each time they approach a new orchestra. Players need to feel this sort of protection as their daily working life is made up of continual criticism, however justified it might be. There is always a 'them and us' situation – management and conductor on one side influencing the well being of the troupe on the other.

In order to redress the balance somewhat, musicians can be quite ingenious in finding escape routes, lightening the pressure of the rehearsal, a witty remark often doing the trick. There must be understanding of each other's point of view for there to be a good working relationship. Each orchestra develops its own character due to the circumstances it faces day to day: the working conditions, number of programmes and recordings during a year, travel arrangements, recovery time etc. Conductors need to hone in to the spirit that emanates from the band. The better the empathy, the better the quality of the music produced!

What follows now is a small insight into some of the circumstances that have led the players to bond in the way that they have. Each experience has helped to make the orchestra what it is today, and produced a distinctive coherent sound that distinguishes this orchestra from any other. This is the basic canvas that is presented to any conductor as he is introduced at the beginning of the first rehearsal of the week.

I remember a performance we gave of 'Don Juan' at the Proms many years ago. Every conductor chooses to start this piece in their own way. It is always open to discussion over how many preparatory beats there will be: one up-beat, or a whole bar – even putting the baton in a position to start can be interpreted as an up–beat. So for this performance it was agreed that by the time the conductor had reached his podium we would be ready with violins up and bows on the string ready for action. As the applause was dying down, the music would begin. Perhaps the promenaders got to hear about this ruse along the grapevine (we will never know) but the applause was too short and the hall deathly silent in eager anticipation of a stunning performance. We did manage the opening flourish after an embarrassing pause but it does go to show that the best laid plans can fall at the first hurdle!

Another occasion during the late 70s at the Proms involved an off-stage band for a performance of 'Dido and Aeneas'. Raymond Leppard had decided to position the group high up in the gods at the Albert Hall. The players had to walk off the main stage during the performance, assemble themselves at the lift and arrive miraculously at the right level in plenty of time to settle themselves in their seats before their entry. All went smoothly at the final rehearsal in the hall, so no-one anticipated a problem. However, lifts at the Albert Hall in those days were rather noisy and were always taken out of commission during a concert so that the recording would not be disturbed. Perhaps management didn't communicate well enough with the staff at the hall, or perhaps personnel changed for the evening, but the crux of the matter was – no lift was going to work for anybody that evening until the performance was over. Racing up flight after flight of stairs carrying a double bass, knowing you had to perform an important solo once you'd arrived at the top - moments like that must really get your heart pounding. And, for once, it wasn't any fault of the conductor!

If anyone mentions the word 'off-stage' there are bound to be hazards for any orchestra and we've had our fair share. Beethoven's overture 'Leonora no.3' has an off stage trumpet fanfare. Providing you know the exact order of the programme this would cause no problem. If not, you might find you are half way through changing into your concert gear when it suddenly dawns on you that the time for the solo is getting perilously close. No-one on stage would ever have known the solo was performed in a state of undress(a pair of black socks, a wristwatch and some lurid paisley y-fronts) until one of our clarinettists had the temerity to catch the whole episode on camera! What are friends for?

The same off- stage trumpeter was also a bit of a joker and decided to liven up a rehearsal of Handel's 'Fireworks Music'. At the expense of the conductor he organised that all the brass section would transpose their version of 'La Rejouissance' into an alternative key, near enough for no one to realise anything was amiss - that is until the strings came in on the repeat!

Another potential hazard lies in Berlioz's 'Harold in Italy'. A string trio has to walk off stage near the final moments of the piece and play chamber music gently in the wings. In a theatre there may well be curtains that can be draped accordingly, but in concert halls there are doors, either open or shut. The doors in the National Concert Hall, Dublin, did not like being ajar for long, and gradually started to close just at the wrong moment. Full marks to the two violinists who nearly ended up doing the splits while valiantly playing on as though nothing was awry!

One feature of the Proms programmes is the insertion of a first performance of a modern work, and this particular year we were given the score of 'Epiphany Variations' by Gordon Crosse. For a special effect, Gordon had instructed members of the orchestra to produce their own set of house keys, insisting that the piccolo player used the smallest set and slightly larger bunches for the lower wind instruments; these were to be rattled at a certain point in the score. His instructions were followed to the letter and our contra bassoonist proudly arrived on stage with the keys from his local parish church. Noisy and cumbersome they might have been, but then you have to expect a wry sense of humour going hand in hand with this type of instrument. The composer was definitely not amused, and no doubt thought very hard before putting pen to paper again!

Yan Pascal Tortelier has his own desire for the dramatic and the unexpected. Respighi's 'Feste Romane' has enough excitement in it for most mortals, but Pascal wanted to go that bit further. A programme involving Respighi's 'Fountains' and 'Pines of Rome' was to close with the exuberance of 'Feste Romane' for a prestigious concert in Madrid. I had foolishly offered to play the mandolin solo in the quieter, peaceful interlude, a fantastic moment in the piece before all the revelries of the festival get

44

going in full swing. What I didn't know until I had boarded the plane was that I might well be separated from the band and have to play my little serenade from somewhere in the circle or balcony, a sort of Romeo and Juliet moment! As it was a popular programme all the seats in the auditorium had been booked in advance and the only space left for me was to perch on a staircase inbetween rows of seats. As no music stand could be found to cover such an unusual situation, the only solution was to balance the music precariously over the edge of the balcony. Not only was I concerned that the music would go overboard, but I was constantly refusing offers of seats from neighbouring gentlemen wondering what I was doing there in the first place. I only wish I'd known enough Spanish to explain the situation properly, so I could then concentrate on the job in hand!

At a time when Pascal was our principal conductor he had a dream of taking us on a concert tour of France as he felt he had never received as much recognition in his own country as elsewhere. He was always referred to as the son of Paul Tortelier in his homeland and not as a worthy musician in his own right. So a tour to France, with the bonus of a concert in Paris, was arranged, and this would undoubtedly raise his profile to a higher level. Everything was going fine until the day to arrive in Paris was approaching. Rumours of a one day strike were rife and which day would the French like to hit? The day of *our* concert, of course! Transport was non-existent, the doors to the hall firmly closed; there was nothing we could do, the concert could not take place. Only once in my career had a concert been cancelled before and that was due to an extremely sudden snowstorm in Britain. Not only did we have to face the prospect of having a night off in the capital city of France, but this was Nov.19th, none other than Beaujolais Nouveau night. Quel horreur! Needless to say, we all made the best of the situation, even though we did sympathise with our conductor, who could only lay the blame on his own countrymen!

Touring with such a large group of people has to have its problems: getting enough seats on a plane, enough hotel rooms, transport to and from the hotels to the concert hall, making sure the instrument van has enough time to get through border crossings and arrive at the right concert hall early enough to set up the stage ready for the rehearsal –these are the headaches for the management. Most of the string instruments travel in specially designed trunkers and there have been occasions when these have been left exposed to great heat at airports whilst on the tarmac awaiting clearance. On other occasions part of a plane has had to be removed temporarily just to get double basses on board. Any damage incurred during transport could make the instrument unplayable on arrival. Moving nearly one hundred people, their instruments, and their baggage around several cities, working in a foreign language and dealing in different currencies requires a cool head and a sense of humour from the management team. These are all made harder when the players themselves are completely exhausted on long tours with concerts every night.

The players have to ensure that they are ready to board the coaches well before departure time, find their way to and from the new concert hall to the nearest restaurant (if they can find one and get served quickly enough in an unknown city every night) and remember the geography of the new hall, what level will they find the instruments, dressing rooms, and actual stage compared to the layout of the previous night. This all happens apart from the stress of performing the eventual concert. Lights on the stage have to be adjusted, seats angled to allow one to move one's bow up and down without hitting a wall or microphone stand - the list seems endless! I have known a violinist's chair leg disappear down a hole in the floor during a rehearsal, and a soloist fall off the edge of a high platform as he turned round to face the orchestra. Luckily both players survived without too much injury but you do have to look out for each other as accidents can happen all too easily.

During the 70s, only principal players were allowed their own room on tour; all rank and file players had to share in order to keep the costs of the expedition to an absolute minimum. One European trip ended in Copenhagen, where we were sharing three or four to a room on make- up beds as all the big hotels had been booked well in advance for a conference and there were no decent rooms left for us. One violinist was explaining how he had turned over in the middle of the night throwing his arms up in the air, nearly making his colleague unconscious. As he was demonstrating the action the following lunchtime a waitress in the hall restaurant in Wiesbaden was unfortunately walking past with a tray full of strawberries and cream. Needless to say all the fruit landed on the floor to everyone's chagrin. In Brussels on the final night of a lengthy tour, we paraded the streets for most of the night as our designated hotel, soon to be demolished, was not the cleanest establishment, and would finally take its occupants, the cockroaches, to an early grave. Our principal cellist at the time, David Fletcher, wryly boasted that he was on the fifth floor – 'Big Game Country'.

Hazards can occur even before you get to your destination. Waiting for the all clear on the runway at Manchester airport before a trip to Europe, it was suddenly noticeable that a plane was about to land on top of us. Our pilot quickly took evasive action and our plane swerved over at right angles on to the grass verge just before the oncoming plane roared past. By the time we had landed at Klagenfurt we had calmed down just a little! On the other hand, during a take off from Brasilia airport we were stunned to hear the stall warning alarm coming from the cockpit. What had caused this I don't know, but again the pilot has to be commended for acting so quickly!

Sometimes events befall us that are no fault of the management at all. One Sunday morning we had to travel to Sochaux in France, the home of the Peugeot factory, a day when coaches were not allowed to travel on motorways. Many bumpy roads later we arrived at our destination to find a shortage of restaurants or cafes at our disposal. This was to be the opening concert of a new hall and we had all been invited to a reception afterwards to celebrate the event. Dvorak 6 was the last item on the agenda and the exposition flowed quite smoothly, Ted Downes in full control. Just as we approached the double bar and the end of the exposition, all lights in the theatre went out. We were in complete darkness and the music finally ground to a halt. An electrician was called and we all waited patiently on the platform for him to repair the fuses. Several minutes later we started the performance once again. We managed the first two pages and lo and behold, having reached the exact same spot, we were plunged into darkness once again! Just before the next play through Ted announced in no uncertain terms that we would continue to play unless darkness reappeared – then the concert would end at that point and we would leave the stage. Five minutes later we did exactly that, packing up in darkness, helped along the corridors by burly fire-fighters happily smoking their cigarettes and then made our way to the reception, held in celebration of the official opening of the new hall!

Management have always made sure that recovery time (that is sight seeing time in my opinion), is organised so that any delay in travel shortens *this* time and not rehearsal time. They cannot be blamed for organising things this way – it is called experience! However, half the enjoyment of touring is to see as many of the local sights as possible, and still leave some energy for the concert. Our trip to Brazil had initially been delayed by many hours so by the time we arrived in Rio we were left with only half the recovery time planned. Our promoters had promised to take us on a tour of the attractions in Rio de Janeiro for those of us wishing to recover from jet lag in a touristy sort of way. The day in question finally consisted of a morning trip to Sugarloaf Mountain in glorious sunshine and an afternoon trip on the funicular to the Corcavado with the statue of Christ overlooking the whole of the city.

Sugarloaf Mountain is a mass of granite and quartz, sticking out of the Atlantic Ocean, 396 metres above sea level. The glass cable car, holding up to 75 passengers, runs from the base to Urca Mountain and then slowly up the side of Sugar Loaf itself, reminding us of the scene in *'Moonraker'* when Jaws attempts to kill 007 in the 1979 film. Having surveyed the scene for a while, you wait your turn for the return of the cable car. Although our first morning in Rio was in bright sunshine, some of our party did get stranded on the mountain for a while as the return journey was delayed because of sea mist! The statue of Christ the Redeemer on Corcavado is the largest art deco statue in the world, nearly 40 metres, made of reinforced concrete and covered in soapstone. You have the feeling that you have entered Gulliver's Travels as the enormity of 'the presence' overwhelms you. If there was any energy left on arrival back at the hotel, there was a trip into the centre of town for a traditional barbeque and evening show.

Needless to say, all members were ready for action on the down beat the next morning, refreshed and exhilarated.

The following day we were invited to the headquarters of H. Stern, the jewellers, who provided a taxi service to and from the hotel. Alighting in the underground car park one is shown through the museum and given demonstrations of gem cutting before being chaperoned into the shop full of glittering diamonds and precious stones. If you succumb to the lure of these exquisitely set stones you had to agree that they would be delivered to your hotel safe at some future date. In fact, for our own safety we were given strict instructions to remove any jewellery we were wearing before wandering the streets of Rio.

Our next venue was Brasilia, the capital, originally laid out in the shape of an aeroplane. On arrival at our hotel we realised that time was of the essence, so we hopped into a taxi straightaway and asked the driver to give us a round trip of the city, which took all of half an hour! One of the most impressive buildings was the Cathedral-Basilica, designed by Oscar Niemeyer (like many of the important buildings there) but the difference being that the majority of the cathedral lies underground, resembling a sunken version of the Catholic cathedral in Liverpool.

Our final performance took place in San Paulo, a free open air concert in a park for the benefit of the locals. About twenty thousand Brazilians were entertained that day in the style of the 'Proms in the Park' which is now a regular feature in Hyde Park, London. One of our violinists became so overwhelmed at the party atmosphere during the performance that he lost control of his bow, which flew into the air and finally landed upright like a dagger stuck into the grass below. As it was such a high platform one of the security guards ceremoniously handed the bow back to the player concerned, in full sight of the cameras and national television!

Flights round the world have made destinations seem much closer in recent years. A tour to Hong Kong in 1979 required much stamina just to arrive in one piece. Violins and violas had to be hand carried, so to get on to the train from Manchester to London required at least three hands –one for your instrument, one for your wheel-less suitcase, and one for your hand luggage! We eventually reached Heathrow in time for a plane to Paris and Dubai; then another seven hours to Singapore, where we had an overnight stay. Hopping into a taxi on arrival at the centre a few of us were given a quick sightseeing tour of the city at night. What a smell of exotic spices in the air! Having boarded a plane the following morning we were disturbed when the pilot made an announcement over the intercom, apologising for good and bad news. The good was that there was not a cloud in the sky at the moment, the bad was that a typhoon was approaching Hong Kong and we might not get there in time to land safely. Sometime later the airport was duly closed and we were instructed to divert to Taiwan. At disembarkation all passports and magazines were taken off us, and after a few hours we were escorted by armed guard to waiting coaches and transported to a hotel somewhere in the hills, used apparently for the amusement of Japanese men! After a meal of a slice of beef covered in a congealed lump of rice with a huge king prawn on top we settled down for the night, wondering quite what was in store for us on the morrow. Without any warning we were suddenly woken by hotel staff bursting in to the bedrooms in the early hours and telling us the coaches were due to leave very shortly. Although Kai Tak airport was still officially closed, the authorities would let our plane land after all. Three bumpy hours later we were eventually seeing the lights of Hong Kong amid very wet surroundings. After queuing for taxis to take us from the airport to the hotel we arrived at the Lee Gardens Hotel to find there were no longer any rooms available - they had been taken over by the staff who could not get back to their own homes! We were provided with a hearty breakfast and gradually disappeared to our rooms during the morning as they became available.

Even after such a journey it was decided that the timing of only the first rehearsal would be delayed - jet lag or not, the remaining schedule would stay the same, and the rehearsals took place as normal. Still, we all made the best of the situation. As soon as a rehearsal finished there was a rush to the exit –we couldn't afford to miss any opportunity for sightseeing, however exhausting it might be! Memories of the Star Ferry, the sight of the Connaught Building (the highest at the time), the view from the top of the Peak, Aberdeen harbour with its Jumbo Restaurant, and the blue waters of Repulse Bay have remained with me ever since.

The days of hand carrying both luggage and instruments have now gone; it can be your choice but there is now an alternative. In the 70s we were giving a concert one night after which we had to board an overnight train. Instruments and cases had to be ready in haste after the concert, players assembling at the station at midnight for the train to make a special unscheduled two minute stop. We lined up on the platform where we expected our numbered carriages to be. The train pulled in to the station on time and slowly ground to a halt. All the carriages had been linked up the opposite way to what we had expected, so we found ourselves all lined up in the wrong place on the platform. Complete chaos ensued. Luggage had to be thrown on to the train quickly through whichever door was nearest. Suitcases, instruments and bodies were all in a tangled mess along the narrow corridors for well over an hour, until the right persons gradually found their predestined compartment. Did anyone really expect to sleep that night?

Being resourceful is definitely part of an orchestral player's remit as the following story will show. In the days of the Berlin Wall if you were performing in the Eastern bloc, you needed to keep together as a group in order to get through the Iron Curtain. On this occasion the management had organised a wake up call at 6am to be received in the rooms of all the players, ready for an early coach and flight from East Berlin to Frankfurt. One player never got his call as the phone to his room didn't work. For some reason, there was no roll call that day on the coaches, so the player concerned was indeed left behind. Hours later the musician, realising he was alone in the hotel, succeeded in buying himself a train ticket, boarding the correct train and arriving in Frankfurt well before the main orchestra! This was quite an achievement in an era before the invention of the mobile phone. Nowadays a lot of texting goes on, management checking on coaches, players, concert halls etc. and players keeping in touch with colleagues and families at home.

Sometimes players can be caught out with time differences from one venue to another. One freelance bass player was so convinced the alarm on his phone was correct he got up immediately, showered and propelled himself down to the breakfast room. Seeing that the whole area was deserted, it began to dawn on him that he was about three hours too early! He reasoned that going back to bed would be dangerous as he would probably oversleep, so he just sat on the steps to the dining room and waited patiently for sun rise!

Crossing the border from East to West and vice versa was a marathon operation. Having a residency in Vienna for a few days would be a bonus on anyone's itinerary and this particular year included a one day trip across the border to Bratislava for a concert in the Slovac National Theatre (which contains a unique chandelier with about 2,500 light bulbs to illuminate the audience). On arrival at the border all passports were duly inspected in detail – no problems there apart from the extra time required. The whole atmosphere was very strained on arrival at the hall – everyone seemingly very suspicious of the western visitors. We had no idea of anything that was on a menu, how to order it, and even what a restaurant looked like from the outside. (Remember that you have only a couple of hours to find somewhere to eat and return to the hall in time to change ready for the concert.) In this case the hall was packed to the beams - all seats taken and the aisles absolutely jam packed. Two Russian soloists had been booked to play the Brahms double concerto and they were understandably nervous. Ted Downes put us through our paces, all going well under control until the finale of the concerto. Suddenly the doors at the back of the hall swung open and a camera crew pushed their way to the front of the hall, positioning themselves within inches of the soloists. This unexpected manoeuvre was made all the worse because cameras in those days needed banks of spotlights in order to film properly, so much light in fact that we were all temporarily blinded! The performance was being broadcast so the playing had to continue and against all odds it certainly did. Most players could play a certain amount from memory until the eyes could focus again and find the relevant bars on the page. We all had great sympathy for the soloists and the conductor!

However, the night was not over until the border had been re-crossed back to the West. This had to be done before midnight if we didn't want to be marooned in no-man's-land. Everything was packed up quickly and we were on our way. The border guards were in no hurry. Not only were passports checked but huge mirrors were wheeled to the sides of the coaches to see if we were carrying any extra bodies clinging to the underneath of the coaches, hoping to make an escape. All this was taking place in complete darkness which was scary in itself. I say naturally dark until one member of our party foolishly grabbed his camera and decided to take a flash photo of the whole scenario. How we managed to survive that night I'll never know!

Another highlight of our professional life was a coast to coast trip across America in March 1995, starting in California and ending in Washington DC. Recovery time on arrival was spent in Disney World, Universal Studios, touring the Hollywood Estates, or relaxing in the hotel. This all sounds more like a holiday, but what followed were twenty concerts in twenty different venues, with a free day in Las Vegas, one in Houston and a final one in New York. Who wouldn't make the best out of this itinerary?

Apart from the obvious things to do in Vegas, it also houses the Liberace museum, which looked close enough on the map for a morning stroll from the hotel. We should have known better and arrived very hot and sticky at the entrance to an amazing collection of cars and extravaganza. Who was more sensible - calmly walking inside from his taxi - but Sir Peter Maxwell Davies! His composition 'Mavis in Las Vegas' epitomises his stay, when reception tried to trace a person called 'Mavis' and the caller really wanted to speak to Max. The subsequent film with Max and a Marilyn Monroe look alike fits the music so perfectly! Max whisks 'Marilyn' away to the wedding chapel where his agent Judy is playing the organ and 'Elvis' is taking the service. 'Liberace' is featured too - all very tongue in cheek and a lot of fun to boot.

A free day in Houston allowed time to visit the space centre where you can have a close-up view of the flight deck and sleeping quarters of a replica of the space shuttle and learn how astronauts handle eating and sleeping in a weightless environment. Free time in New York has to be divided between sight-seeing and shopping. Our son, who was eleven at the time, flew out to join us for the last few days of our tour, his beaming face appearing next to a guard in front of Macy's, the Empire State Building, the Statue of Liberty and finally the top of the World Trade Centre.

Weather, like border crossings, can also cause untold problems for both instruments and players. A trip to Ouarzazate in the middle of the Moroccan desert in May 1994 for the launch of 'des Symphonies du desert' was obviously going to involve a fair amount of heat during the day, and we were advised to spend a maximum of ten minutes in the sun on the first day of arrival. As the plane circled the airfield to make our landing we were aware of a drumming noise coming through the sound of the engines. A display of local talent had been organised to welcome us and they had formed a large circle on the tarmac, all wearing national costume and hitting huge drums with long pieces of hosepipe. The display was wonderful and lasted about 40 mins along with a demonstration of traditional dancing (some of our own players willingly joining in). Already we had been exposed to too much sun and we hadn't even left the airport! The concerts were to take place outside in an acoustic shell, the first of which was situated in front of the Kasbah de Taourirt. This meant closing off the main six lane highway to traffic for the whole day as row on row of chairs were arranged on hundreds of rugs, no doubt on sale in the markets only days beforehand! Closing part of the M60 or M25 would cause havoc back in England, but as very few cars used this particular highway as a normal rule traffic jams were not a problem. The city was originally a customs post on an important caravan trade route between the Sahara and Marrakech, but more recently achieved fame as a backdrop for films like 'Lawrence of Arabia', and 'Gladiator'. During daytime the heat was oppressive but as the evening wore on the temperature dropped considerably and the wind was sufficiently strong to send the music flying all over the town. That's when our concert was due to start! A few days later, at the time of the final concert at the Kasbah d'ait Ben Haddou, the mixture of extreme heat and cold had affected most players, so much so that there was a continual queue of desperate players waiting their turn for the one portaloo positioned discreetly behind the acoustic shell. A performance of the Berlioz Overture 'Roman Carnival', Brahms' violin concerto, and Tchaikovsky's symphony no.4 saw players performing their solo and rushing off the platform in agony. Illness had besieged the majority of the band, and we were lucky to perform the programmes with a quorum of key players at any one time!

Heat also caused a few problems with instruments in Oman, but as we were guests of the Sultan and the concert hall was in our hotel complex, no one was going to complain. The main problem we found was sitting on the stage for over an hour before the Sultan arrived for his special birthday concert. Security reasons were given for this rather strange phenomenon, but here we were again racing each other to the nearest conveniences as soon as the concert was over. The New Year celebrations and general ambience of the hotel in such a lovely balmy climate soon dispelled any uncomfortable feelings during the performance!

Bahrain was another country where we were looked after exceptionally well. We were asked to play the national anthem before the concert and when the parts arrived they were for a military band only, highly decorative as the individual parts were. My husband and I agreed to provide some string parts, manuscript paper being photocopied for the purpose. We added a few arpeggios to make the parts interesting, hopefully with enough decorum to provide a regal performance. We were unaware that time was of the essence on the day of the concert, and one short play through at the end of the rehearsal was all we would have before the official rendering. We dearly wanted someone from Bahrain to win a medal in the Olympics to see if our recorded version was still in existence!

Heat is not normally a consideration for the Orkney Music Festival that takes place in June. A few of our players offered to drive a van from Manchester up through Scotland and then on to the ferry to Kirkwall so that a good number of us could have the pleasure of riding bikes on the island, exploring more of the terrain than we could within the confines of Kirkwall. I remember pedalling hard against the odds on a bicycle in full concert gear, in the rain and almost going backwards because of the gale force winds! A trip to the Isle of Man many years ago was also hampered by rough weather. The orchestra flew in to the airport with no problem. The choir from Oldham decided to use the ferry, as did a few of our players, who wanted to appreciate the fresh breezes on deck. The weather was so severe that the ferry was able to dock only after many hours of waiting out in the bay, all occupants missing the whole rehearsal of 'The Dream of Gerontius' with Bryden Thomson, due to be performed later that evening. Those who had been on board seemed to sway left and right through the entire performance as they attempted to keep their balance and concentrate on the music rather than their seasickness.

Sometimes staying in a port can have its advantages. Palma in Majorca was our last destination after a two or three week tour of Europe and we were all looking forward to a mini holiday before returning home. Our visit coincided with the return of the fleet from the Falklands and the Ark Royal was one of those berthed at the port.

Some of us were lucky enough to be invited on board for lunch with the captain, and were given an escorted tour of the ship, in return for some tickets for our performance that night.

Receptions for the whole orchestra happen very infrequently as they are understandably an expensive event for the host country. I remember being invited for a drink of pink champagne on the lawn at 'Czechers', the British Consul in Prague, and in the town hall of Belfast, after a prestigious concert with Günther Herbig. We were all invited to sit down at long tables, the mayor of Belfast duly entertaining Günther during the whole proceedings. Although Günther's understanding of English is exceptionally good, the addition of a strong Irish dialect was too much for him, and he was noticeably struggling more and more to follow the conversation as the evening went on. This particular tour ended rather momentously when our coaches were treated to a police escort to get us back to the airport in time!

Language problems can affect the most erudite of musicians. One of our double bass players was renowned for window shopping during any free time, as he was determined to buy something for his wife that was typical of the region, whatever that might be. On a visit to Lindau, on Lake Constance, he entered a particular shop, admiring the dresses on the rail. The assistant asked if she could help, so he proudly announced in his best German 'My wife in England, she is twelve!' (meaning the size of clothes he was looking for). My husband, being as helpful as only he can be, added 'Lolita!' in a low voice, before escaping from the shop rather quickly. I don't think many souvenirs were purchased after that.

One of the main perks of the job is to experience as much as possible of the local flavour and tourist attractions of the city, wherever it might be. Sept 2004 saw a short trip to Merano and Verona, but staying in Bolzano, which lies close to both centres. Romeo and Juliet's balcony in Verona is world famous, but it occurred to a few of our well informed group that a morning free in Bolzano would be an excellent opportunity to see the South Tyrol Museum of Archaeology with the display of the Neolithic Iceman called Ötzi, along with his clothing and possessions intact, all kept at a constantly low temperature. Plenty of incentive to get up for an early breakfast that day, for sure!

We look forward to visiting Mannheim, especially if we have a free morning available to visit the Luisenpark, one of the most beautiful parks in Europe. There is a large lake in the centre with electric gondolas tracing a submerged track round the edge, so quietly that the lives of the huge trout and carp remain undisturbed. Stopping at a café for refreshment, we happened to choose a table overlooking a small pond. The noise there was indescribable but very loud, and very mystifying. We had appeared just at right time for the mating of the many lake frogs, the main inhabitants of the water!

Japan has many exciting things to offer, one of them being a ride in the shinkansen, the bullet train speeding past Mount Fuji. There is so little vibration on board that one could upend a pencil without it falling over. One of the concert halls in Tokyo lay alongside Ueno Zoo, famous for its pandas, well worth a visit! Performing in Yokohama, the second largest port, a number of us rushed to the Landmark Tower after the rehearsal to experience the view from the 69th floor as the sun was setting over the harbour and the Bay Bridge, a mere 2,800 ft. long. Half the fun of this escapade was travelling up in the express lift moving at 2,500 ft. per minute. For something completely different we have experienced the calm and serenity of Sapporo in the north where the concert hall was situated in the middle of a park. All great memories to savour for a long time. We actually gave the first performance in Japan of 'The Planets' by Holst in Nov 2004. It was such a great occasion that every member of the unseen choir came down on to the stage in full traditional dress during the applause to shake hands with the conductor, Pascal Tortelier.

Our tour to South Korea in March 2008 started on the south coast on the Tongyeong peninsula, the port often described as the most beautiful in South Korea. Our hotel was situated on the sea front, with breathtaking views across the bay from bedrooms having plate glass windows down to the floor, an under floor heating system permanently on, and very substantial doors of solid steel for whatever reason we could not imagine. The guide books write of a small dock busy with ferries and fishing trawlers, omitting the fact that large container ships pass through in the middle of the night with some very effective horns. Local delicacies include clams, oysters and molluscs, and the fish swimming in tanks outside the cafes can be selected for a meal if you so desire.

Seoul came as a complete contrast, staying in the luxury of Lotte World, (Korea's answer to Disneyland). The hotel there is part of a huge complex of shopping malls, underground shopping arcades, and a glass-covered amusement park with a bridge leading to an adjoining island with a magic castle in the centre of the lake. A running track has been laid round the edge of this lagoon with the occasional loudspeaker along the side of the track gently issuing strains of Max Bruch's violin concerto to entertain us as we were completing the circuit.

Our lasting impression of South Korea came with an incredible dancing display in colourful national costume performed in our honour and accompanied by hourglass drums and clanging gongs for us in front of the concert hall in Gumi, a town just north of Daegu in Gyeongsangbuk Province, the city destined to host the 2011 world athletic championships. After the evening concert we were back on the coaches for a long drive back to Seoul ready for the flight home the following day.

Our visit to China came unexpectedly during the New Year celebrations at the end of December 2008, so we were playing in The Cube, which is right next to the Bird's Nest

Stadium, and in The Great Hall of the People in Tiananmen Square only a few months after the Beijing Olympics had taken place. The chance to experience the enormity of Tiananmen Square, a walk on the Great Wall of China, the fantastic water jet display in the swimming pool of the Cube (computer controlled to the music of Tchaikovsky's 1812 and switched on during the interval of our concert) - who would turn down an invitation like this?

The Far East seemed to have far more western signs in place since our first visit five years earlier; it was much easier ordering food and generally finding our way around. Gone were the plastic meals advertising what was available in the restaurants. Instead of pointing to these, one could now take a guess from the menu, even if some of the translations were a little suspect. During our first visit one of our members picked up his plate at breakfast time, warming it in the microwave as was the custom. Proudly sitting down in the middle of the management team, he then discovered he had no food on the plate at all, it was all a plastic model, showing what choice there was available! This was the same person who had persuaded us to share two bottles of wine among the three of us on our first night in Japan. After a long haul flight, we didn't need much persuasion, and the drink was in fact very enjoyable. When the bill came, we realised why wine does not readily appear on Japanese menus. The cost was prohibitive! We all had an enforced diet for a few days so we could get through the rest of the tour in a more sober fashion!

All these sort of experiences join together to make up the character of an orchestra, and explain why there seems to be a united front against the new face on the podium. We have lived through conductors like Brian Priestman shouting furiously to amateur choirs hours before a performance, and then turning to our front desk players muttering 'It's only done for a purpose!' Raymond Leppard caused strife when he wanted to get on with a rehearsal calling out 'Come on dears, put your knitting away!' His rendering of the Radetzky March, when he had forgotten how many repeats we had already played and was left conducting thin air, did redress the balance somewhat, though I have to admit his performances of Bach and Handel were always momentous occasions. Tod Handley would be as happy discussing the length of batons as he was on the intricacies of English music. As a protégé of Sir Adrian Boult , perhaps he would not have been surprised to learn that during a performance of 'Job' by R.V. Williams at the Proms, his mentor had leant so far forward on the rostrum that his baton was actually brushing the head of the nearest second violinist, namely my husband!

During the 1960s John Hopkins was well known for saying 'We just need to work on a few odd spots' without realising that one day he would turn up for a rehearsal suffering from a sudden outbreak of measles. We've had conductors who have managed to double the length of Sibelius 2 ; Walter Susskind intriguing us so much we could easily sit with fiddles on knees completely missing our next entry; and finally Aaron Copland conducting 'Appalachian Spring' and the ballet music from 'Billy the Kid' saying 'You're trying *too* hard, my music is not *that* good! Just relax and play it!'! If you add a performance of Messiaen's 'Turangalila' symphony given in his presence for a special birthday celebration, firework displays seen from the roof of Tivoli Gardens, Copenhagen, or across Lake Maggiore in Italy; or New Year's Eve parties in Oman and China; performing in the beautifully maintained Musikverein in Vienna; or working with and depending on some of the best desk partners one could wish for, and a leader like Yuri Torchinsky who will regularly thank his section for their team work in the concert hall - perhaps this job has not been so bad after all!

4th Mov. : FINALE: ALLEGRO MAESTOSO
WITH VARIATIONS
The mystique of conducting

The excuse to talk in an informal way with many of the conductors who have re-appeared year after year, yet always from a safe distance, has been a fascinating challenge. The fact that they were prepared to give their spare time was one thing, followed closely by the panic of knowing exactly what questions I really wanted to ask. One expects that the maestros themselves spend much of their time in deep thought, either poring over a score or delving into the background of the work involved. Most players spend their time just trying to keep their standards as high as possible, and in juggling a career, home ties and a social life, which sometimes does not lie very well with the strains and unusual working hours of an orchestra.

'Time to stand and stare' really does not come into a player's diary! Yet, for the conductor, this sort of preparation is absolutely essential for the underlying raison d' être of his calling. The musicians guarantee to perform the notes on the page, as long as the man in charge can produce the link between the sounds produced and the composer's original intentions

So, here we are, both involved in interpreting the music written on the page, but from completely different angles. This dividing line has to be there, otherwise chaos would follow, which is why we have had many tyrants on the podium in former years. Ruling with a rod of iron was generally more acceptable in those days, and problems can occur more frequently now as players have more scope for discussion and possibly more input into the performance as a whole. That is not to say that the final word doesn't come from the podium, but it is expected that there will be a certain leeway now that never would have been allowed in the past. Of course, this is to be welcomed (the alternative is unthinkable) but this does put more pressure on the conductor, who now has to justify his opinions more than ever before

With this in mind, I wanted to discover whether today's conductors felt intimidated by the prospect of being a solitary figure against the might of the masses. I know we are subservient to the conductor in the final performance, but the feeling of immense interest and elation can spread like wildfire during a rehearsal as indeed can intense boredom and frustration. The following discussions took place in many situations - hotel lounges, with Strauss waltzes playing over the loudspeakers; sometimes conversing over the telephone; and others were in the green room between rehearsals. This all added to the fun – the extra ambience of unexpected door bells, orchestral call bells announcing the end of a break-time, or the general bustle of a hotel lobby. The interviews appear in alphabetical order, which seemed the fairest way, and I hope they give an insight into the various characters and idiosyncrasies of each mentor. Each one has brought something special to the life and workings of the orchestra and proved to us that there are many ways of interpreting the dots and dashes on the page. Vive la difference!

MARTYN BRABBINS

One of the tutors for 'I want to be a conductor', Martyn studied with Ilya Musin for two years at the Leningrad conservatory. He went on to win the Leeds conducting competition in 1988, and has himself initiated a conductors' training course at the St. Magnus Festival, Orkney, where he hopes to give pupils the chance to make mistakes and learn from them before they walk in front of a professional orchestra. He has also written informative articles on the experiences of conducting. As time was of the essence, he agreed to talk over the telephone one evening in May 1999.

What are the difficulties facing young conductors?
'The problem about conducting as a novice conductor is 'What do you actually say to the orchestra? What have you got to give them?' That's what lets so many of them down. They are so daunted – as we all are! In the face of the skill and the expertise and musicianship, it is very hard for the young conductor simply to get on with it – in that situation. That particular workshop could have been improved with perhaps some sessions before they hit the orchestra, and possibly a bit more input along the way, but that's for another day. I think it's a very sad thing that the 'Young Musician' has lost its subsidy - the things like the composers and the conductors' workshops go first. These just don't get such good viewing figures.

The personality of the conductors didn't come across easily because they were all so terrified, and orchestras don't really understand this. Well, they probably do, but the orchestra situation is a terrifying one; there is a crowd element in there - you are in the same boat and powerful as a unit, and therefore it's quite a terrifying thing to stand in front of. You have to learn how to cope, how to talk to the orchestra collectively, and to individuals. This really is an incredible skill. If you have a really good technique and you can therefore communicate musicianship (if it's worth communicating) then that can sort of counterbalance any fear and trepidation that may be coming across as a weak personality.

I do strongly believe that conductors ought to be highly trained. I don't think in this country that there is a long term, properly structured training course. Maybe the Royal Academy is getting there, with their three year full time course. That's quite reasonable. My experience was in Russia, and if you didn't do the full course of five years then you didn't qualify. That is not to say that you couldn't get employment. The training there is very intense, and for a long time. Often the students have already done a four or five year graduating course, so there are very few young students of conducting. Fully rounded acceptable young conductors are very rare, and a lot of what passes for competence and genius is actually just flash in the pan, with very strong media hype machines behind them. Orchestral musicians see through them very quickly.

I feel that conducting isn't really a young person's profession - you need to experience a bit of life, and have a serious bout of training in what you are supposed to be doing. Of all the musical skills, the responsibility on the conductor is greater than on any other. A solo performer may be a close second. The conductor is responsible for recreating the great works of art. It is an incredibly onerous task and shouldn't be taken lightly in any sense. And that is what worries me. If someone's young and has done quite well, that's marvellous, but it's not necessarily enough to be quite sustainable. Time does tell – let's put it that way! If you're a real genius, say, like Simon Rattle, you must have had incredible gifts of communication at a very early age.

There has to be a sacrifice to achieve anything. My personal sacrifice was spending two years in Russia and leaving behind my wife and security. I was doing fine as a player, but you've got to put yourself through hoops before you can say you've worked hard enough to get the chance even to conduct. The getting together of players and trying to form my own group never appealed to me. I had a sort of shy lack in self-confidence when I was younger. I wouldn't have asked people to do that sort of thing because I would have expected them to say 'No!' I was very fortunate with the route that I did pursue, it paid off, and I was fortunate enough to win the Leeds competition. Of course, this gives you a kick start and I realise that it doesn't happen to everybody. There's no career structure, everyone approaches it from a different angle. You think about things in a different way, you study with different people - it's something you can't pin down. I just spend all my time working, preparing. If I've got time off, I'm always conscious that there is stuff to prepare for. If I'm away from home, I spend all that time away swotting, reading, listening; that is almost all the bulk of my activity really. I do more hours preparing than actually rehearsing and performing. That's something most people probably do not even understand.

Orchestral musicians may not quite appreciate that you can't just stand up in front of an orchestra and hope to get by with just your wit; it's just not possible. With repertoire that the orchestra don't know then, possibly, but with the German repertoire that Günther Herbig is talking about, then even more so. That is something that I hope I'll grow into. Of course, I love conducting Brahms and Beethoven, but the thought terrifies me, in a way. I hope it will come in my old age! I don't find that a problem, because these are recognised as great works of art. Conducting should be a very serious undertaking – you can't just jump in and think 'I'm a bright, lively personality, therefore I can conduct.' There has got to be a lot more to it than that. That's my gut feeling, probably because I studied with someone who took it incredibly seriously and showed me what his approach led to – it really is a religion out there. It is cut throat and difficult there as it is here, even though the training is so long. Training is most rigorous, not just in Musin's class, but all of them. It is much more structured; there are classes in bowing, orchestral technique, ear training classes, language classes, if you want. It is taken as seriously as learning the violin, and why shouldn't it be? You can play in fourth position, so why can't the conductor conduct in seven eight?

The Leningrad school of teachers was founded by Malko and continued by Musin. Rabinovich and Mariss Yansons teach there – it is quite a serious business. As you can see, it's not done by would-be conductors, but people who really know what they are talking about. Music education in Russia as a whole is something that is a matter of life and death. They work hard and practise to a far greater extent than the students do here, in my opinion.

I think conducting is an interesting area to look at, because it is really taken for granted at some colleges and, as you know, orchestras suffer! This isn't as it should be. People get terrible health problems through bad conductors. Whenever there is a statistic about orchestral stresses and strains it is very often the conductor who has caused them more than anything else. After that, it's just a lack of competence, I suppose you'd call it. I think, in the workshop, they wanted more of the teaching element in it, and providing the video idea would have been useful. I do hope another workshop will be organised soon, because, sadly, there are so few of them.'

HARRY CHRISTOPHERS

Known internationally as founder and conductor of 'The Sixteen' as well as guest conductor for many of the major symphony orchestras. It was after one of his sessions with the Phil. in May 1999, that we talked about his introduction to the world of the conductor.

'I ended up studying music at Oxford after changing from classics. While at Oxford, singing had been my life, having been a chorister at Canterbury. I was also a wind player, a clarinettist, so I carried on with that, playing in the chamber orchestra and things like that. There came a decision in my last year at Oxford, that I couldn't do both, so I concentrated on the singing side of it. I was introduced to early music and in particular the renaissance through my tutors Bernard Rose and David Wulstan. Ever since then I have concentrated on early music, renaissance and early baroque, then I tend to jump to the 20th century - I don't say I neglect everything in between. After Oxford, I was offered a job at Westminster Abbey, staying there for six years, and through that period I formed the choir. I have my own views on what has gone wrong in years past, and what was wrong with the cathedral system and the grand choral tradition. So I began to develop The Sixteen. However, I had to live so, after the Abbey, I joined the BBC Singers for three years which was an absolute means to an end. Luckily, the manager and conductor of the BBC Singers knew that I wanted to conduct, and they were desperate for tenors, so they let me off for every bit of conducting that I wanted to do.

During that BBC period I made use of the time watching Boulez, Rozhdestvensky, Ozawa - all those greats. I learnt how to do things and, more importantly how not to do things! Still, my area of music was going to be the early. In essence I wanted to bring the heart back into choral music, rather than just cross the 't's and dot the 'i's. Our great choral tradition has got rather obsessed with perfection – everything has to be perfectly in tune, perfectly together, all the consonants in the right place and spat out rather unnaturally. I always remember the words of a critic who said,

Harry Christophers. Photo by Tom Bangbala

after hearing King's Cambridge, that he didn't realise the word Egypt had four syllables! For me, at that time, it didn't matter, as long as there was a performance which touched the heart of what the composer wanted. To take the music that was for church services into a concert setting one had to do something extra to bring the emotion to the audience. Later, I formed the orchestra of 'The Sixteen', a period orchestra, watching very closely what people like Ton Koopman had been doing. I was feeding off them really because they were so very stylistic, but if there is any criticism of the continental baroque specialists it is that they are so interested in style that they tend to forget what the whole work is about. Any Bach cantata or Handel oratorio came to be singled out into little movements of stylistic beauty but, in the end, there wasn't any sense of continuity.

I'm not completely soaked up in the early baroque traditions with 100% stylistic things. You cannot put everything that you do with a period orchestra into a modern orchestra. There is that element of compromise. I've always felt that the detail one has for the baroque music, attention to harmonic detail and what the composer wrote, has stood me in good stead for music in the 20th century. Basically, they are incredibly similar - it's everything in between that gets in the way!

I find the 19th century very hard because the rubato is incredibly difficult to judge, for instance in the Grieg piano concerto. It's another area of music that I love listening to, but I don't absolutely feel that it's in my blood. I can take everything up to the end of Beethoven perhaps into Brahms and feel that there is an element of music developing out of the baroque. From early Brahms onwards you've got such a different change in the whole concept of music for that space of 150 years until this century, when everything is beginning to harp back to earlier times. It's trying to get to the heart of all these composers, and I firmly believe that no one conductor can get to the heart of everybody. I tend to perform works that I know I can offer something, and add little tit-bits to. So that's the basis of it!

What worries me with so many symphony orchestras is that they just don't listen to each other. This is the fault of the big symphonic repertoire and the enlarging of all the symphony orchestras, where people get behind a stand and feel safe, and cease to be personalities. The notes are on the page, so you just play them. For baroque and early classical pieces, though, the bass line is the basis for the harmony and you need to shape each note. You can't teach that, or mark it into a copy – each crotchet having a different stroke, it has to be felt - the musicians are all individuals and need to play as such. With all the jokes that fly around the BBC Phil., the whole orchestra is full of life and taking on board things, whereas with some other orchestras there seems to be such boredom there, a certain unwillingness to make beautiful music sound beautiful!

With baroque music and a symphony orchestra they'll book an organist rather than a specialist continuo player, so they play in an unimaginative way and don't spark the cello section. That individualism has just got to come out of the music. The orchestras that concentrate on contemporary music are so much more aware when it comes to the earlier classical music. Raymond Leppard reintroduced Monteverdi to this country with a really lush string sound. He made a big orchestra sound wonderfully alive and energetic. His recordings are still excellent, but to a purist way of thinking they weren't really continuo-based. Still fantastic for their time!

It is really difficult for a modern orchestra to do baroque music now, due to the physical nature of the instruments. I feel sorry for modern brass players having to play Bach orchestral suites – it is so different a sound. The trumpets are now built to get to the back of the concert hall; trumpets in Bach's day were like a first oboe. You see that from a lot of Purcell's work. In the turn of the century it was put down as two trumpets. We look back at the original and it was put down as trumpet and oboe. Bach's trumpet parts are just a nightmare because the little modern trumpet is so loud. It is a wonderful exercise to play a Mozart or Haydn symphony and to say Haydn is boring is probably due to the static and heavy way it was often played, certainly in the first half of the 20th century. Those parts that you had for Beethoven 7 were done by Breitkopf when certain phrasing and articulation had come in as the 'norm' and this was how it should be played. If you go back to Beethoven, half of those markings aren't there.

I do try to allow my musicians freedom to express themselves individually – it's my job to mould the whole. As long as singers and instrumentalists know where the shape of the phrase is going, the musicians must have a sense of using their innate musicianship, and they are familiar with me, so they know exactly what sort of thing I want, and the way I'd like to shape a performance.'

Sir Andrew Davis CBE. Photo by Tom Bangbala

SIR ANDREW DAVIS CBE.

Chief conductor of the BBC Symphony Orchestra from 1989-2000 and a champion of British contemporary music, especially Sir Michael Tippett. This discussion took place in 2009.

You studied with Franco Ferrara in Italy. What aspects of conducting was he concerned about?
'I did go to study with Ferrara having been at Cambridge for four years, and summer courses at Canford with George Hurst, who was marvellous for foundation and technique, I have to say. Ferrara didn't teach technique as such. I went to Rome for a year so I could study with him rather than to Vienna with Hans Swarowsky, who was the other famous teacher because I would have been there for three years and I was too impatient. So I chose to go to Ferrara and I certainly didn't regret it. Up until that year, he'd had a small orchestra – members of the academia orchestra, which was a very good orchestra (well, not great then but much better now). But they were professionals and they ran out of money so we worked with students instead. Half the time there was no oboe player, so the first oboe part was played by the flute, and the second was played by the clarinet who couldn't transpose the part very well, so it was very chaotic. Indeed, very Italian! So that was a little frustrating. Occasionally, I couldn't get something together so then I'd go to him and say 'Why couldn't it be together?' and he would say 'That's because you are doing so and so!' So he would work with technical things if you asked him to. I was with him for eight months, and learned most from the six times he actually conducted the orchestra. That was a revelation!'

I understand that he would only conduct a few bars at a time.
'He was very frustrated, because after 20 bars he would pass out! He had a very extraordinary career; he was very successful at first and then he really would pass out at concerts. There were various theories, one of which was that he had epilepsy. I just think he felt the music so profoundly, his body wouldn't take it. Whatever it was, it was a great loss because he was a very powerful man,

strong and everything very centred.

It was interesting because we studied operas as well. I'd come from King's College, Cambridge – I knew about 'Stanford in G' but didn't know the 'Barber of Seville', which was the first opera we worked on, so that was great! Sometime later he asked 'What would you all like to work on next?' Straightaway I said 'Lulu', not realising that, with Ferrara, music stopped with Stravinsky's 'Firebird'! But he was very inspiring, demanding and rigorous. The four years I had already spent at Cambridge working every day with David Wilcocks was also very good, because he was a real perfectionist and wouldn't let anything go.'

You were in charge of the BBC Symphony for a long period of time (1989-2000)
'I almost made my professional debut with them, but I think I had previously done a concert in Leeds with the BBC Northern and Leeds Festival Chorus. 'Toward the unknown region' by V. Williams, a piece that I actually adore, was on the programme and it was the first time I'd ever done it.'

We used to have a player who was a good caricaturist and used to draw the visiting conductors on the orchestra folders so that every so often you would see the same face reappear. That's how I remember you coming to conduct all those years ago!
'I didn't look quite the same then - glasses, no beard, and a Beatle haircut. Someone from the Los Angeles Philharmonic, the first oboe in fact, was a keen amateur photographer, who took a picture of me around that time and I showed it to my son about three years ago when he was about 16, and he had no idea know who it was! Anyway, the first really big thing I did was when the BBC Symphony Orchestra were performing the 'Glagolitic Mass' and they were without a conductor at the last minute. I learnt the score in about four days, and that was the beginning of a long association with them. In the meantime I went in 73-74 season to Toronto and was there for thirteen years. That was really marvellous and I still go back there every year. So it's about 37 years I've been in contact with the Toronto Symphony Orchestra. It's nice to have that continuity and the fact that I go back to the

BBC Symphony Orchestra too. I'm conductor laureate of both my orchestras and I like that because very often a conductor finishes his stint with an orchestra and disappears.

I spent 1988/ 89 with BBC and Glyndebourne and it was a fantastic time. I reckon to have had the two best jobs in England, in an opera house that received no public money except for the touring company, and then for the BBC which was all run by public money. The result was that they were both free to do exactly what they wanted in terms of repertoire. So there was much more variety here than with orchestras who tend to do their Beethoven 5 and Tchaikovsky 4ths. I remember doing a concert with the BBC Symphony Orch. and they played Beethoven 5 which they hadn't performed for about 12 years!

In 1997, my predecessor in Chicago, Bruno Bartolett, who had been the music director of the Chicago Lyric Opera since 1956, decided he was going to retire in 99. So I got a phone call from a friend of mine, Matthew Epstein, who had been artistic consultant there for many years. Actually, my wife, who is American and was a coloratura soprano and now runs our young artists' programme, saw Matthew in New York and he said 'Oh, Bruno is going to retire, it's too bad that Andrew's going to be too busy.' 'Well, you don't know till you ask him!' she replied. 'Well, don't tell him anything!' he warned. So she phoned me straightaway!

I had conducted there five times already and loved the company. So, the next day I got this call from the general director of the company. 'Is there any chance you'd be interested?' And of course I'd already decided I wanted a new start as I'd been with Glyndebourne and the BBC for 12 years. I've just done my first 'Tristan' so it's enabled me to do all this wonderful repertoire after probably the shortest search process in the history of music - within a week! That's how it should be!'

Who gave you your first break?
'The first orchestra I should thank is the BBC Scottish because I was there for two years in 1970-1972. I had a contract to do 40 concerts a year and ended up doing about 50! This was new repertoire for me, but of course they were very sweet. Of course, I

wasn't untalented, I suppose, but they did put up with a lot of things.'

You need an opportunity like this in order to learn.
'Yes, that's true and of course they had that position for assistant conductor for quite a long time. Colin Davis did it when he was very young, as did Simon Rattle and Chris Seaman.'

Do you find American orchestras very different from British ones?
'Toronto was another wonderful experience. When I went there I had to learn how North America works, in terms of chatting up sponsors etc. In those days about a third of the budget came from ticket sales, a third from fund raising and a third from the government. The third from the government has shrunk of course since then. In America we get nothing from the government but we get something from the national endowment for the art, which pays for about three pairs of shoes! Toronto is a wonderful city. Again it was there where I did my first Mahler cycle - over nine years!'

Was Chicago a difficult proposition in the aftermath of Solti?
'Solti of course was with the symphony orchestra and was a very dominant part of the scene there, but he had gone by the time I arrived. Valerie still goes there to do some fund raising things because they have a foundation, and I'm involved with that as well. The two most prominent conductors of the Chicago were both Hungarian, Solti and Fritz Reiner. The main story about Riener was when they were on tour and had two programmes, one opening with 'Oberon' and one with 'Don Juan'. He came out on to the stage and thought it was 'Don Juan' so he gave this whacking downbeat instead of waving at the first horn. And one cellist entered with the arpeggio opening of 'Don Juan'. In the interval Reiner called him to his room and said he was fired. 'But maestro, excuse me, but you made the mistake and I was the only one who came in.' 'It was not what you played but the *way* you played'. It's probably cock and bull but it's a nice story! Chicago is a great theatre city, with lots of theatre companies. Sometimes we work with them and I do work with the symphony orchestra pretty regularly. I bailed them out a few times when Daniel was ill.

Everyone there is very excited by the arrival of Muti. I know him a bit, so I'm looking forward to perhaps spending some time with him. He used to cultivate this 'arrogance' but now he's so much calmer.'

You were principal guest conductor of the Royal Stockholm Phil Orch (1995-98) along with Paavo Jarvi?
'Yes! Paavo and I were both principal guest conductors and there was no principal conductor, so it was a bit unsatisfactory. A wonderful city and a good orchestra but we only spent about five weeks a year there each so that is not really enough to make a big difference. When there is a Principal conductor and you are the guest, then you can just go and have fun.'

And music director of Glyndebourne (1988-2000)?
'And Glyndebourne too! I first went there in 73, John Pritchard asked me to go, and I loved him so much! He took me out to lunch at Wheelers restaurant in Soho, saying, 'I'd like you to become my assistant and do two performances.' I said to him that I was really thrilled but I had no experience of opera at all. 'Oh, we know that. What you'll find is there are more things that go wrong in opera than almost any other field of human endeavour.' This is typical! But when they all go right, there is nothing like it and that sort of puts it very well. I am constantly being reminded of both these aspects really.'

Did you have a musical background?
'To answer that I must relate a story about when I was 12 or 13. The trebles of Watford Boys Grammar School, of whom I was one, went up to Studio 1, Maida Vale, to sing the narration part in Vaughan Williams' 'Hodie' which is a piece I still have a very soft spot for, and Vaughan Williams himself was there. This was a year or two before he died. He came and congratulated us afterwards, although most of the time I think he was asleep up in the gallery! He looked so like all his photographs – a big baggy man with white hair - he was very sweet to us. The interesting thing was that this was the first occasion I had seen anything like an orchestral concert. I had grown up in Watford, and hadn't

started going to the Proms by then. The LPO came to Watford three times a year and I used to go there, but this was the first time I had been in a recording situation with a live orchestra , and the first time I realised that an orchestra *might not like a conductor*! I thought 'Why are they behaving in this obstreperous way?' I don't know if I learnt any lessons from that or not.

When you are a young conductor it is hard, but if you know what you are doing then an orchestra will basically be nice to you. I took part in the seminar for young British conductors in Liverpool in 1969, a two week course run by Sir Charles Groves, whom I knew, because Jonathan, his son, was a chorister at King's College, Cambridge when I was an organ scholar. He was such a gentleman and very generous and helpful to young conductors. I remember conducting the 'Firebird Suite' and at the end of the Infernal Dance I think I asked the bass trombone player to play a little softer! I should have known better! Anyway he said, 'Mr conductor, I've played this for Igor Stravinsky and he liked it fine this way!' Of course, what I should have said was 'Oh well, if it was good enough for Stravinsky it's certainly good enough for me!' instead of something stupid like 'But I'd like to hear the violins!'

I do remember the first time I ever conducted the Chicago Symphony, which has a very famous brass section. This was in 1974, when I'd been at it full time for about four years or so. We were doing Dvorak 7, and Dvorak is always difficult for balance. We started the first movement and I said something rather smart like 'The brass section of this orchestra is justly world renowned but I'd like to hear the rest of it!' Actually I must have done it with such a smile and charm that there was suddenly a great shuffling of feet from the rest of the orchestra. It is sometimes touch and go. When you're younger there is this natural resistance, because you've got people who've been playing for years and years in front of you. 'What's this whippersnapper going to tell *me* about Brahms, when we've done it with Bruno Walter?'

I used to find more difference in reaction in different countries. I used to think that Germans liked to be *bossed* around more and Italians liked to be *indulged*. This is still true but I don't feel it as much now, maybe because orchestras and their

78

personalities have changed and I feel more confident in myself; if I'm not self-assured at my age then I'm in big trouble! I'm always nervous when I go to a new orchestra and I haven't been here for about 35 years, and even for the opening night of 'Midsummer Night's Dream' at La Scala! We had done a public dress rehearsal which was absolutely full, which had gone very, very well, and sometimes if the dress rehearsal goes well I feel very nervous. I suppose that if one didn't feel nerves then one might as well give up, actually! The trickiest challenge is to use this positively, and that applies to all of us.

I found that when rehearsing Britten with the La Scala Orchestra (which is very good), the style was not right, especially for 'Midsummer Night's Dream', which is very delicate - with these funny little glissandi things that are very hard to do right and by the fourth orchestral rehearsal you wonder if it is ever going to get better. Days like this you say to yourself 'Why am I doing this? At my age, my father had been retired for three years!' But of course, we have a lovely time; I'll probably be like most conductors and just keep doing it.'

At least you can. With us, there's going to be a cut off point where we cannot play anymore.
'I wonder if that should happen with conductors too?
Sometimes I think I'll do a little bit less and give myself some time off, but then something else comes in. I was asked to do a lot of operatic projects with La Scala, Barcelona, the Met, and of course opera takes a long time. Then you think, 'Oh, I'm not doing enough concerts', so you cram them in only to find that you don't have a holiday. However, I went to New Zealand for three weeks and took my 19 year old son with me. I think it's like England 50 years ago, and I loved the Fifties! I was very happy growing up then, they were very innocent times! There were the remnants of all this patriotic stuff around [pointing to the Elgar scores we had just recorded] which was rekindled by the war, and then the 60s came with all the protests and cynicism and our entire little world was shattered!'

Any designs on training others in the future?
'I would like to spend some time teaching. I've had a couple of people who have worked with me privately, just looking at scores, picking my brains for musical ideas and so on. The only time I have actually done a course was when people stood up and conducted something and you criticised or helped them or whatever. I think I'd really enjoy doing that on a more regular basis. I have been asked to be the Artiste Associé for the festival in Besançon. They have a big conducting competition there every other year, and in two years time I'll be the head of the jury for that. A lot of quite famous people have won it and it's such a nice place – a French provincial town, with some mediaeval - a lot of 18th century buildings that are very elegant. It's almost surrounded by a river, and there are a few vineyards and superb restaurants! 'We'll pay you so much for your accommodation and all your meals.' That's OK with me!'

On what basis do you accept engagements?
'If somebody wants to pay you a lot of money you tend to go there. If it's an orchestra you like working with the music will be satisfying and another reason is to explore the surroundings. There are parts of England that I really don't know. So I once hired a car and had a nice little holiday in Shropshire which is quite lovely, but is quite a secretive place. Do you know the Vaughan Williams 'Wenlock Edge', the song cycle for tenor and piano quintet, the setting of the words of A.E. Housman? He also wrote in his poem 'A Shropshire Lad':

'Tis a long way further than Knighton,
A quieter place than Clun,
Where doomsday may thunder and lighten,
And little 'twill matter to one!

So I stopped in Clun, a very quiet place indeed and had my sandwiches by the river!'

What is the future for classical music and/or training of conductors?

'People have been saying the symphony orchestra is dead and that opera is ridiculous. It is a worrying time. We are in a fortunate position in Chicago because I think we are the only American opera house that does not have a deficit. The big problem at the Met is that they had a huge endowment fund that they can take the interest off but, because of the stock market, the whole value of this thing has dropped so low that they can't now use it because of something in their bylaws that says if it loses a certain percentage of its value they cannot draw on it, so they really are in a pickle. It's a hard time because a lot of people unfortunately think of us as a luxury. If you buy two good seats for a whole season's subscription of eight operas, that's quite a lot of money. I happen to think that what we do is too important, and I don't think people want to lose it. It's not just entertainment, it's much more than that; it is spiritually very important, I've always felt that. We just have to keep doing it and make sure that what we do is compromise. We have a set for the second act of 'Rosenkavalier' where there's the presentation of the rose and there are these curtains with what looks like little castles on them all the way down. Actually they are plastic spoons! But you can't see that from the audience and they look wonderful. Another designer would have wanted costume jewellery. No, I think we'll survive!

With young conductors, there is someone who I have helped a bit who became principal trombone in the Chicago Symphony Orchestra. He was 19 when he got the job, but we didn't know his age because in America you are certainly not allowed to ask anyone their age, to prevent discrimination against older people. This is good, of course, especially as people always play behind screens for the first round. He's now called associate conductor in St Louis and they are giving him lots of things to do like children's concerts.

I must say that when I started I got lucky because I got the BBC Symphony Orchestra concert with the 'Glagolitic Mass' and that was just before I started work in Glasgow in 1970. At that time Pierre Boulez was the conductor of the BBC S.O. and also the New York Philharmonic. William Glock was still at the BBC and he must have been singing my praises to Boulez because the first orchestra I got invited to conduct in America was the New York

Phil! So within 18 months I had conducted the New York, the Philadelphia, Chicago, Boston, and Cleveland. At the time I really thought I was dreaming all this and I also felt like a fraud. I mean I've got over it, because when you're young you do. Some of what you do may be immature but you hope it has enough energy to carry it through. At the time I kept thinking that this was ridiculous. All the same I had fun. But when you get older, the same with everything in life, you get reflective and sometimes you lose your way a little bit. I've seen it happen - it's a bit like a mid-life crisis. Eventually you get through it and get enough self knowledge or something. It's not just self confidence, it's experience and knowing what you have to offer. Someone might conduct Bartok better but won't conduct Vaughan Williams.'

You mean each person finds their own niche.
'When I started out various people said I must specialise in something. I remember Thurston Dart, who was a professor at Cambridge during my first year there, calling across to me one day 'What are you going to do with your life, Mr Davis? I replied, 'I'm going to be a conductor!' 'Come to my house tomorrow and have a sherry.' I remember we drank lots of gin rather than sherry but basically he said I had to find a specific area and concentrate on that. I thought that was boring! I wanted to do lots of different repertoire and maybe I was very lucky. You need to be lucky at a certain point; you need then to be able to make use of it and, anyway, I must say I've had a great time!'

SIR EDWARD DOWNES CBE.

Ted was a father figure for the players of the BBC Phil for many years, taking a very strong hand in supporting us when we had to go through the musicians' strike in the 1980s. Peter Leary, chairman of the BBC orchestras' committee at the time recalls how he was invited to Ted's house when the union meetings were taking place in London. 'I will never forget the enthusiasm with which he joined us when we undertook "unofficial concerts" during our brief severances from our BBC duties.'

Andrew Orton, occupying a seat on the first desk of violins for a decade or two, relates how, in the green room, it wasn't a question of discussing what was going to happen in the piece we were rehearsing, it was more of 'How are you and your family, and their family, and is everything all right?' 'He and Joan were more interested in you than in what was going on. If Ted was telling a story about Covent Garden or the singers he would start off and his wife Joan would finish and vice versa. It was never a question of 'Oh no, you're mistaken!' – *that* was the story! They were so amusing, you sometimes forgot that you had to go back to work, and the office would have to put the bell on to remind us. 'Come on, off we go!'

Andrew goes on to describe two little anecdotes regarding his association with Ted, the first one showing the great humanity of both Ted and Joan.

'Six or seven years ago I was organising a memorial concert for Ray Lomax, a dear friend of mine, who used to be a member of this orchestra, and of course the first person I could think of who I would like to conduct this concert was Ted. So I rang him up, and he said he would love to do it, but the programme might be a problem.
'Mozart Requiem'
Don't know it!
'Vaughan Williams 'Serenade to Music'
Don't know it!
I then said the overture 'Nabucco'
'Great, I'll do it!'

Sir Edward Downes CBE. Photo by Tom Bangbala

So what Ted (a guy of 78 years old) was really saying, in spite of his being in the middle of dress rehearsals for some big opera at Covent Garden, was that he and his wife Joan were prepared to drive up to Manchester on their one and only free day, just to conduct an eight minute piece, and I thought that was absolutely fantastic!

The second one concerns a performance of the 'Alpine Symphony' which I happened to find myself leading, with Tom Bangbala sitting next to me. Of course we were enjoying getting stuck into this rehearsal with Ted and this particular bit was either depicting climbing up the mountain or coming down, and concerns a soloistic triplet passage, tickety boom, tickety boom, tickety boom.' In a strong Yorkshire dialect, Andrew continues 'There's me and Tom going hell for leather throughout all this section and when Ted finally stops conducting he turned and looked at us both. "You two are supposed to be a cool mountain stream. You sound very much to me like a hydro-electric power scheme!"

Ted and Joan never travelled apart from the orchestra on European tours, always preferring the camaraderie near the back of one of the coaches, plenty of laughter ensuing. His wife Joan was always at hand and, queuing for breakfast one morning, whispered to my husband, who was next in line 'More toast, Gromit?'

My first ever rehearsal with the BBC Northern, as it was originally called, was with Ted and an animated production of 'Le Nez' of Shostakovitch. (Reminiscing with Ted in June 2009, he admitted he had photocopied the original score and made his own translation, which is the reason we were able to record it at all in the early seventies.) I cannot describe how scared I was at the time, and how desperate I was at not coming in spare, but Ted's general attitude did inspire me and I did make a commitment that *this* was the orchestra I wanted to be involved with. Later productions for Radio 3 included Wagner's 'Die Feen', Das Liebesverbot, 'Rienzi', Strauss's 'Friedenstag, and Benjamin Britten's 'Paul Bunyan', hardly ever performed at the time, but great for a radio audience. The room was full of well known singers, but Ted showed no mercy. If you made a wrong entry, sang the wrong notes or rhythm, Ted was not known for mincing his words! He would then wipe his glasses on his green towel, and demand the red light to be switched on again. All recordings would go to the last second, in the hope of achieving a better take. His interest was always Russian composers and large canvasses of Wagner and Verdi, and he would always tell us the story behind all the works we were playing. If he didn't manage to include naughty nuns in his story line then we all thought we were missing something! Ted chose to conduct the Leningrad Symphony for his 70th and 80th birthday celebrations. What might he have chosen for his 90th, I wonder?

Yan Pascal Tortelier vividly recalls a telephone call he made one morning to ask Ted how to manage the various beatings in Elgar's 'In the South'.

'Ah! Pascal,' he said in his distinctive voice:

'Beginning in 3– at 6 in 1 – at 8 back in 3 etc....' Pascal says he did not even have a chance to ask him about the slightest ritenuto or diminuendo! His final memory of Ted and Joan was at an almost surreal New Year's Eve party, 1995/96, which took place in the sand dunes just outside Oman, after an invitation from the Sultan to present concerts especially for him and his guests, when Ted and Pascal opened the procedure by dancing with each other's spouse.

Here is a transcription of a telephone conversation Ted and I had one evening in April 1999, discussing workshops and posts of assistant conductors.

'For many years, Mr Jorma Panula has been the teacher of conducting at the Sibelius Academy in Helsinki. Among his pupils are virtually all the Finnish conductors – Esa-Pekka Salonen, Jukka-Pekka Saraste, Osmo Vanska, and Sakari Oramo. I've encountered him on two occasions in Holland, once for the Kondrashin competition. He is a lovely, amiable man who clearly knows everything about this whole business of conducting. His comments, which various people were listening to, were very to the point, very humane, not ultra-critical – he obviously is a kind hearted man and a very good musician. In this Kondrashin competition last summer, I think, they could accommodate 18 people to come to Holland and they had something like 150 applicants of all nationalities. In order to weed them out, they all had to send in a video of themselves conducting something or other of their choice, and in May, that is precisely a year ago, about five of us from the judges went to Holland for a week and we watched 150-odd videos. We whittled them down to 50, and then down to 18. Then there was a week in the Concertgebouw with the Holland Radio Philharmonic Orchestra (which is a very good orchestra indeed) going through the motions and we finally got a winner. Mr. Panula was, in a sense, the best of the judges. Another one of the judges was Mr. Sanderling, whom you probably remember. That's about all I can tell you about Mr. Panula!

Many orchestras used to have assistant conductorship posts. It was not usually any sort of competition but, twenty or thirty years ago, almost all the orchestras, including the BBC orchestras, had a young assistant conductor. In Scotland, for example, it was Colin Davis. After that, when the chief conductor was Christopher Seaman, the young conductor was Andrew Davis, later to be chief conductor of the BBC Symphony Orchestra. The reason they stopped doing it was possibly a financial one – one never knows. It is actually an ideal way of doing things. I have known it happen in America. The conductor of the Cleveland Orchestra was a man called George Szell, for many years a terrifying conductor but terribly competent. They had a fund whereby, every year, they would provide for a student conductor to go over and sit in on rehearsals, occasionally conducting matinee concerts and things like that.

Two or three years ago, I did a seminar for a couple of weeks in Holland with various young conductors, and I think I worked with ten eventually. This was not a competition. The first week we worked with two pianos (they conducted the pianists) and we worked for about six hours a day. The second week we had an orchestra, the Radio Philharmonic indeed. They went through their paces and I tried to make suggestions and help them. We did two public concerts, one in the Concertgebouw and the other in Utrecht. Although it was not a competition there was a special prize awarded to the one whom I thought was the most promising; not the one with the greatest achievement, but the most promising. I awarded it to a young German chap who has since been appointed as an assistant conductor to the Radio Philharmonic in Holland.

It seems to me that it's a wonderful idea to have someone who can sit in rehearsals like that. If the chief conductor wants to do it all by himself then it is a problem, as many of them want to conduct as often as possible so they can actually learn the piece they are doing, if you know what I mean! So there are many reasons why conductors might not want someone to help, though I'd have thought it was a wonderful idea, I must say.

When I started, there was virtually no way to succeed unless you went to an opera company and you became a repetiteur. You just hoped that some conductor would break his leg just before a performance and you could go in and conduct! You'd have no rehearsal, of course. When I started at Covent Garden, for the first three or four years I never conducted a rehearsal; I conducted plenty of performances, but I never had a chance to rehearse them. This sorts the men from the boys!

There was another way of getting in, but that was a very rare one – that's the one that Beecham did. Tommy Beecham's father was, you know, Sir Joseph Beecham, the chap who made Beecham's Pills and got very rich. When Beecham was about 16 - 18, his father asked him what he wanted for Christmas, and he replied that he wanted the Hallé Orchestra for a week! So that's what he had, and Beecham did his worst and learned all sorts of things. Another way, and this is someone you probably remember, was that of Raymond Leppard, who had some very influential friends, one of whom bought him a series of concerts at the Festival Hall! There are also these conducting competitions, of which there seem to be a lot nowadays, when the prize includes a series of concerts with various orchestras around the world. Nowadays it seems much easier for a young conductor to get started than when I wanted to start.'

Günther Herbig was explaining recently how he knew people in America who wanted to become conductors, but they could not even get in front of a professional orchestra; they've been trying for about twenty years!

'That in a way is rather extraordinary! There are in fact hundreds, and I mean hundreds of small orchestral societies all over the United States. They do very ambitious concert seasons and in places that you or I have never heard of. I'm just thinking now of Dennis Simons, former leader of the BBC Phil. He went, as you know to Canada, and conducted first in Calgary, later becoming the 'king of music' in Winnipeg. These concert series are all over the United States in towns we've never heard of. You've heard of Orlando, Mickey Mouse land? They have one of the best and biggest concert halls I've ever seen in my life! We had a packed audience and had a standing ovation. That is in Orlando, a name you do not associate with a cultural centre. That's why I'm quite surprised that these young potential conductors haven't got in on that sort of thing.'

Apparently over a hundred applicants have to be whittled down by looking at their C.V.s
'One of the great dangers when you read these C.V.s and then encounter the people is you simply cannot believe that they are the same person. Some of them, you think, must be Toscanini's deputy! But they stand in front of a band as though they have never done it in their life before! They will put down with whom they have studied and I frequently find they have studied with me and I've never heard of them! What they have done is dropped in on a rehearsal. That is categorised in their C.V.s as having studied with someone. This seems to be common practice to do with this C.V. business. But I've just remembered something – one of the people who was in that symposium a couple of years ago, an Irish-American, applied for one of these jobs in the United States. One was in Pittsburgh, and one was for Houston, in Texas, I think. He got a job as an assistant conductor, and I wouldn't have given it to him, for God's sake. It entails helping whoever the chief conductor is, and also doing a series of concerts. So there are jobs around there. Look! Basically, if you've really got something, you'll find a way to display it. In the opera business I am encountering all the time lots of young men who think they have the right to stand up at Covent Garden and conduct 'The Ring'. They think they've just got to sit down there and the chance will come to them. They are not good enough – that's perfectly obvious!'

The initial standard of the workshop shocked us so much as an orchestra; we realised that our future depended on situations like this and perhaps there was some way we could help.

'It is clearly in your interests in the long term. The only way you learn to conduct frankly is to conduct, even if it's only two people, or in a pit band. You can study all the theory, but you only find out how to conduct by actually doing it. The fundamental thing is that a conductor himself can't make any noise at all. He can grunt, but that won't get him far! He has to persuade or terrorise, or force, or charm a group of people in front of him to produce the goods!

The thing about conducting is that you cannot hide anything. When you get up there and make music, you're really doing it with your trousers down. I mean, you can't conceal *anything*!'

It was in June 2009 that I started an email correspondence with Ted and Joan, mainly to ask their permission for this taped interview to be printed, and also to reminisce over Ted's last performance with us in the Bridgewater Hall of Shostakovitch 7 in celebration of his 80th birthday. There was an electric atmosphere that night. Ted's eyesight had deteriorated very badly, but he was not fazed by this, in fact he seemed more determined than ever to achieve the utmost out of all the orchestra, conducting from memory but with great vigour, never missing a single cue and giving such a wide grin when the resulting sounds really pleased him.

Having agreed that I could 'print and be damned!' the final email ended with a request to send their very best wishes to all the 'old guard' in the orchestra and how they missed coming to see us. Nothing prepared us for the sudden news the following week, that their lives were now over – and nothing will ever diminish the memory of working with such a great and enthusiastic musician.

Sir Ted and Lady Downes in Oman. Photo by John Wade.

Sir Mark Elder CBE. Photo by Tom Bangbala

SIR MARK ELDER CBE

Protégé of Ted Downes; MD of the Hallé Orchestra since 2000.Conducted Last Night of the Proms in 1987 and 2006; long association with English National Opera; conducted at the Met in New York, the Bolshoi in Moscow, the Marinsky in St. Petersburg, the Hong Kong Philharmonic and the China Philharmonic, including a performance in the Forbidden City. This was a discussion in July 2009.

I've been in the band here since 1972, but I think you have known Ted Downes a bit longer than I have. How helpful was he in the early stages of your career?

'That's right! Well that was the year that he took me to Australia – Jan 3rd. 1972, with everything that I possessed because I didn't know what I was going into. I took 13 tubes of Colgate because I didn't know whether they would have any there, and every LP that I possessed, because in 1972 I was about 24 and was only just beginning to be aware of things outside my own little family background. Ted did something for me that nobody else at that time could have done - he gave me the opportunity to learn who I was. He didn't want me to be another him; he wanted me to be me, but I was so young and needing experience and I didn't know if I would be ever be able to become a conductor.

That was one of the reasons I took his advice when he offered me the chance to go out and live in Australia because it was an apprenticeship for me. I knew I had a job at English National Opera when I got back, whenever I was ready, so I went out there to see whether I could find enough confidence to do this very demanding job. I think that by the time the two and a half years were up, I thought 'I'm ready to give this a go'. Those two years in Australia were very formative, very uncertain sometimes. I made a lot of mistakes, I did things I shouldn't have done, I said things I shouldn't have, but Ted was always there supporting me in his sort of bluff, direct, down to earth way. I was immensely grateful for that - and of course I am still.

To be talking about him now after what's happened is just

93

so unexpected. The Hallé were all in your studio last night with the chorus and I just talked about him. He didn't have a relationship with us, yet he had spent years in that studio and I suddenly thought - nobody had said anything to the Hallé about him. They probably don't understand who this man really was, not just to me, but his strengths, his determination and amazing ability to rise above his background. So I just talked about him. He just helped me at a time of my life when we all desperately need somebody to help. Just to say 'Go on, you'll be fine', 'Get on and do it' and he gave me an opportunity by taking me to Australia.

So I was there for two years, because he was the director, and when he had to come back to Europe I was still there to take on all the shows. If I had stayed around in Europe I might have got a few performances here and there but I did 160 performances in two years. You know if you play an instrument every day, you play a bit of chamber music and play in orchestras, you build up to it. With conductors, the orchestra is there - you can't develop. All this business about being in front of the bathroom mirror – that's nonsense! The only way you learn is by standing up and realising what didn't work - so do something different. Make your technique adjust according to what you are hearing and what you want to hear. And he gave me that. I couldn't believe it when he said to me (I was on the staff at Covent Garden) 'Well laddie, once you've found your feet and you haven't fallen off the podium, you'll be conducting two or three times a week.' And I thought 'It can't be true, because that doesn't happen to a young conductor, how do English conductors get their experience?

It has had an enormous effect on me for the rest of my life. I've never forgotten how much gentle support he gave me. He never said 'No, no, no, you must do it in two!' He said you'll find it easier later when you've done a few performances. 'Get on with it, and keep at it, and work hard', and that's why I try what Ted told me with these young conductors, so having the assistant conductors at the Hallé makes a very important part of what I believe in. Orchestras are very tough on young conductors. Of course they don't like not having experienced hands, but unless we do this the country won't ever produce better and better conductors. I wish more orchestras took this responsibility more seriously. You find that every orchestra tends to start, but as soon as it goes wrong or there are money problems, then they say 'Get rid of that!' But I think it should be one of the most fundamental things.'

Well, our workshop here was ten years ago and although we were going to have a number of them they haven't as yet appeared on our schedules!
'That's classic! In Newcastle, the same thing has happened. The players said that they didn't want the same mistake to be made again.'

Everyone's profession in the orchestra is reliant on the conductor. It's a two way thing.
'If an orchestra feels that it can't give of its best because the conductor is in some way stopping that because of his own tension, nerves, lack of experience, lack of musical intensity, that's very frustrating.'

Their heads are on the block as well of course!
'It's one of the things that a young conductor has to learn to cope with, how to show respect and encouragement. To me Ted was a rock that I felt I could trust and rely on, and I must say that after a time it became a little frustrating. He was so solid that when he repeated a performance he repeated it - you must know what I mean. I was impulsive and wanted to get on and find my own path. I hoped for something more experimental and magical, but that wasn't his way and I knew that at the time and I thought to myself: there's some strength here that I need to observe and respect and of course I learnt an enormous amount from him, which has never left me. I feel terribly sad that I wasn't able to say goodbye. I have never denied how much I owed him and I think he knew that. He was so grateful, so thrilled at what has been happening with the Hallé - that I had found my feet as it were.'

I think you have done for the Hallé what Ted did for us. He was always fighting for our cause.
'Exactly! He was, because he was a player himself originally, and

he knew that if the music director didn't fight then no one else would. If the management don't feel that the MD is fighting for the orchestra then they think that they don't have to either. It's a very important position and also for the public too - a bridge between the orchestra and the public, building a relationship with the whole community.'

Manchester has the best concert hall in Britain, according to Sir Charles Mackerras!
'Charlie said that, did he? Well, I say this all over the world. The Chicago Symphony say to me that when they come on a tour of Britain, Manchester is their favourite hall. That's really good to know, isn't it?
What I like in Manchester is the relationship, the feeling between the platform and the public.'

I don't like high platforms, especially if you are playing near the edge. You are more concerned about what is going to fall over.
'Quite, it's psychological, isn't it!'

I'm sure Vassily Sinaisky saw the first performance of Shostakovitch 4 in Russia in 1961, and I think you were present at the first performance in London in 1963 also with Kyrill Kondrashin conducting?
'That is fascinating, isn't it? Shostakovitch was very important to me. When I was young I became very excited about the sound world he made. And by sheer coincidence a great school friend of mine and his dad invited me to this concert because Oistrakh was playing the Brahms, not because of the Shostakovitch. So I was very thrilled to see Oistrakh live and then I looked at the programme and saw Symphony no. 4. And I thought 'Oh well, that will be interesting'. I had no idea how important it would be for the rest of my life. Isn't that incredible!

We travel round the world now, but I had never seen a group of Russian people before and had never heard Russians playing their own music. It was incredibly exciting for that reason because I didn't know what to expect from this symphony. And I had no idea it was the first time it had ever been played in London or its history. I just remember sitting there watching this enormous orchestra cram on to the stage at the Festival Hall with this huge bass drum player with one leg, having to walk up those stairs with one crutch. There are climaxes in this piece that are the loudest climaxes in the repertoire and I can remember the sound of the music, the opening, rum, chum, chum, chum, that rhythm and then that fugue which of course you've played many times. And I'd never seen or heard anybody play as fast as that. It made an enormous impression on me, the double timpani at the end going on and on for ever and ever and the quiet spooky, frightening ending.

There is a lack of clarity about the first performance in the U.K., Pam. Kondrashin did indeed do it at the Festival Hall (this was the prime piece that had been put aside in 1936) but Gennadi also got hold of a score and came to the Edinburgh Festival with the Philharmonia and my memory is that the performance I heard was immediately *after* that done at the Edinburgh Festival and so it was the *English* premiere I heard. Obviously it was an incredibly important work for them to bring to the West, given its emotional content. I'm dying to do it here in Manchester, but Vassily got there first in the Festival.'

There's room for both, surely.
'Well, it is such a great work. Do you enjoy playing it?'

Well, not the ending, if I'm honest. After you've played your heart and soul out you then have to be so quiet and delicate. I look through all the Mahler symphonies now to see which ones have the quiet endings! I think you have to save something for the end of these epic pieces because they demand so much concentration. If your heart is beating too fast, you just cannot get through the final bars.
'You mean you need to have the control at the end?'

If you have a long exposed note to play at the end and you get a slight bow shake as it gets quieter and quieter - it really is quite frightening.
'And of course Shostakovitch knew what fear really was. What he

97

was experiencing in Russia at that time, living every moment of his life in fear, we cannot even imagine. I immediately bought the studio recording that Eugene Ormandy made in the early 60s.'

It's hard to understand that it was not possible to get Russian recordings over here at that time.
'No! My whole understanding about Russian playing, traditions and style came from when I worked in East Berlin, which was much later. Then you could buy these Russian recordings; they came out from Moscow in lorry loads, and I bought an enormous amount of them, hiding them in my suitcase to bring them home. I still listen to them and look at them. It was a way of my making some contact with a very different style of playing. Not just a horn vibrato but the way the whole brass sound was, the way the conductor interpreted (to my taste still now to extremes – either too fast or too slow - there isn't any moderation). But it has a sort or rawness to it and an intensity of emotional commitment that is very un-English. He is still an important composer to me - he would be on my list of special composers. And as the years go by I find more beauty and importance in his music, which one doesn't always find in composers as time goes on.'

You spent quite a while in the opera house in Sydney!
'Of course! That's when I got to know Charlie Mackerras. He came out to open the opera house for the Queen. He did the 'Magic Flute' and I took it over from him.

Did he tell you that the day the opera house opened it was unbelievably windy? Sydney harbour is a wonderful venue but there was this whole platform outside so that everybody could be seen. The Queen was wearing a lime green suit and boater hat and she spent the whole time trying to keep her skirts down! And they had this enormous barge in the harbour that was covered with a net, and under the net were hundreds of coloured balloons. Obviously once the ceremony was over it was going to be like an enormous daylight firework display. They were going to take off the net and all these balloons were going to go all over the harbour. You wouldn't believe what happened. The wind was so strong the guys got half the net off and the wind took the whole thing, the whole net and all the balloons, and within 30 seconds they were on Mars! The whole thing disappeared into the sky! It was so funny!'

Very impressive!
'Yes! But it was a great thing for me to be involved in the opening of a new building, something that has become a recurring feature of my life. I did the first subscription concert in Birmingham; Simon did the opening concert and then he went away and I did the next week. So I was there right at the moment when the audience was beginning to listen and be aware of their orchestra in a different way. I was there in Sydney; I was there in Adelaide for the opening of the new opera house, just before the Sydney one. Strangely it is in a place called 'Elder Park' and the conservatorium of music there is called the Elder Conservatorium, as the Elder family was one of the twelve families from Europe who founded Adelaide. Elder is a very common name in Edinburgh and the Lowlands of Scotland where you never have to repeat the name. In America, my wife and I pronounce it Elderrr, otherwise they think it's spelt Elda.

Being around new concert halls and new theatres has been a strangely recurrent feature of my life and I've enjoyed it enormously. I'm interested in the way an audience and orchestra are together and the space in which they interact is a very big part of the experience which the audience and orchestra have. That's why this new Festival Hall is so important to me, to see whether or not it's going to improve the orchestral experience in London. But I love the Bridgewater Hall in Manchester. I love playing in it, and I love working in it and that has something to do with the temperature. For a conductor when it's slightly cooler than the orchestra really wants it's perfect, because you don't get too hot. And I'm always very relaxed here and that gives me confidence.'

You certainly notice the difference when you rehearse something in the studio and then go to the hall. You hear so many different things; things that have been such a muddle suddenly become clearer.
'Absolutely right! I think the role of a conductor goes way beyond

conducting. With an orchestra for a long period of time in a community this inner life is very important. Of course there are so many types of conductor and there are different ways of building relationships, first with the orchestra themselves and then together with the public. Then as a spokesman for the orchestra for the people who raise money, who give money, the people who believe in the orchestra and want to know more about it, and the people who don't understand the importance of an orchestra in a community. And the players themselves have an amazing capacity to answer all these questions, to be part of it. I think one of the things that we've developed here in Manchester is the orchestra's experience and skill at being vocal, being aware of how important their personalities are. I said right from the beginning I wanted characters in this orchestra; I didn't want everything to be bland. I love the fact that you have different personalities and you should feel that you could give your character to the way we make music together. My job is to unite it, to give it integrity and to say, 'Don't stick out, but have courage about your character' and when we are appointing players it is important to have personalities. People who have an interesting take on the way they play their instruments, and their attitude they have at being in an orchestra, so that they feel that the future of the orchestra is in their hands as much as in mine or the managements, and that we are all trying to do something together.'

This is probably very different from fifty years ago when the conductor was up there on a pedestal and the players were kept down at an inferior level.
'I know! I think that's right! It was the abuse of that relationship, Pam, which started the idea of the musicians needing to have a union - to support them and control them. Having just been in Chicago for a few weeks - that was the city where it all started - it is amazing what things go on. I'll give you one quick example. The opera orchestra in the Lyric Theatre has very substantial breaks as many orchestras in America do, but in addition to that they have negotiated an extra two minutes to get from the orchestra pit to the orchestra's relaxing room, which is 15 paces away.

If the conductor does make a case for his orchestra and champions them and loves them in the way (and love does not mean in a weak way; if you love them then you want them to succeed and you do everything you can to make them better) then I think there is a chance that people will understand the point of an orchestra, that it has a role to play in everybody's lives - it's not just something that happens to be there. You want to support it because it gives you something that you cannot get any other way and that of course is the joy of live performance, because you are sharing and creating something. Two years later you may do the same piece and do it completely differently. Let's hope that one can develop and improve on it.

I think that the role of an MD is different from that of a guest conductor. Some of my colleagues don't want the responsibility; sometimes one has to have very difficult conversations when someone loses their quality and something goes in their playing, or they lose their embouchure - that is so difficult, and they don't want the responsibility of facing these problems. But I take it as part of the whole - cherishing and developing an orchestra in a community. And in that aspect Barbirolli was an inspiration. His personality was so different - he had that sense of belonging and knowing that the orchestra needed his leadership. He was very committed to them. He made something from nothing. My situation historically was very different, but what was so fulfilling, and encouraging for everybody, was that the orchestra and I managed to get on together quite quickly.'

Have you any suggestions for the training of conductors in the future?
'It's incredibly important for the lives of orchestras. In Germany every town the size of Manchester has its own opera company and there you have a chance to offer opportunities to young conductors. And the opera houses in Germany and Austria are like the football leagues are here. I mean they have a third, second and first division, so you can grow through the system. There are a number of British conductors over the years who haven't had the experience over here and they have gone to live in Germany and

become enmeshed in that system. We will never be able to offer that system which is why, like in America, I believe every orchestra should have its resident assistant. The orchestra accepts that the help and training of a young conductor is part of their brief. I think mature conductors have a responsibility to do what they can to find ways to inspire and instil the right aspirations in other young conductors. What Ted did with those master classes in Holland I do at the Royal Northern College of Music. I'm professor of conducting there so I go whenever I can and talk to the kids about conducting, about what sort of scary things the conductors go through, so I don't just shout at them. I make it a two way thing, which produces a completely different atmosphere. I always say this:

'I bet there are one or two people in the orchestra here who think that one day they wouldn't mind trying to become a conductor. You should all think about it. What is this conductor doing? You learn the piece to be able to play it and he uses this time for his practice. You have your instrument but his instrument is the orchestra.'

Is it important to get children involved through singing?
'You are so right that singing is fundamental to us all.

There are so many different religions in school now that people are very nervous about having school assemblies as we used to know them that they cancel the singing. It is so important that singing gets *back* into children's lives. We need to show children that music exists in many forms and that they have a natural propensity for it. I really believe that we all have music in us and it's a question of how one gets it out while the children are young so that they understand it is part of them at a time when there are other things that are starting to compete with their time. Television and all that is now a huge danger! They can always come back to it even if they leave it for a while, but if they have never been given the chance to feel and hear music...

I recently received a letter from an 80 year old in Oldham, who said she was lucky enough to be taught music by William Walton's brother. She used to do 20 minutes of theory and then he would play little snippets of classical music, just to whet the appetite. 'And that's how I've learned to like classical music and I've never looked back!' I get a lot of letters like that!'

And if you can get children singing young enough, they are not at all embarrassed.
'If we can harness that energy, get every child to feel that it is natural, they'll *want* to do it. It's OK that they will go off and do other things, but it's been awoken inside them. You have to start at primary school where the teachers need to have confidence about music.'

Are they getting the training to be able to do it?
'I used to be on the board of an organisation for a long time that helped primary school teachers to find the way to include music in their work and we found that the kids were never a problem, the head teachers were never a problem, it was the teachers themselves. *They* were very nervous. 'Oh no, I couldn't possibly do that!' I do hope that we can change this in the future somehow!'

TECWYN EVANS

Tecwyn Evans during the performance of the celebration of the moon landing anniversary. Photo by Andrew Price

Chorus Master at Glyndebourne in 1999; the first New Zealander ever to conduct at the Proms in 2007; first conductor and deputy chief conductor at Graz Opera in Austria, 2009. This discussion took place in between rehearsals in Nov. 1999 of a scientific oratorio celebrating the 40th anniversary of the moon landing.

'My real background is singing; my father is a singer, my mother a chorister and I sang in choirs since I was ten years old. There is no established tradition of producing conductors in New Zealand, I only have two significant predecessors, Warwick Braithwaite and John Matheson, both associated with Sadlers Wells and Covent Garden respectively at least 30 years earlier.

My early break in the business in New Zealand was when I applied to be a composer in residence to an orchestra - I had done composition at university. This was a job where I could write music for the orchestra as well as conduct the first rehearsal of all their concerts. So I was doing all sorts of stuff with an orchestra before I had had any real training. And because I was the only one of my time doing this I got to do all that was available to me. So I just stumbled into conducting, it was the furthest thing from my mind prior to this.

As my weakness was the orchestral side I needed to come out of my comfort zone. In a chance conversation with Simon Carrington, from the King's Singers, he suggested I went to Kansas to study with a great English guy called Brian Priestman. Through the Fulbright scholarship I stayed in America for one year but learned enough for five years with all the stuff that was thrown at me. When I arrived there Brian Priestman said I had a very bumptious attitude. I'd been a big fish in a small pond having had many opportunities to conduct already, and finding myself in front of two pianos - I didn't think it was going to be that beneficial. I might well have suggested that, later to realise my big mistake!

So maybe sometimes you think you are more important than you are, but it's that confidence that helps drive you. To me, the art of conducting was more about the reaction I got from the people I was working with rather than me standing out in front of people. My first ever conducting in NZ was when I was 23 and three years later I was chorus master at Glyndebourne, so I did feel things had moved on quite quickly.

I arrived in Britain after my studies in America intending to hide my choral background but, having been offered the job of chorus master by Sir Andrew Davis, I would have been stupid to refuse it. I learned how an opera house worked, and how to learn scores in a short time.

For my first 'Boheme' I had only 40 minutes' rehearsal with the orchestra and cast before the performance, and for my first 'Meistersinger' recently in Graz, it was straight into the performance! In some ways this 'German system' is perfect because there is so much going on, there are so many opportunities - the orchestras are used to the music because they have played it for so many years, so it is not surprising there are more conductors coming out of that system than elsewhere. I decided to leave Glyndebourne after four years; I made the finals of the Leeds Conducting Competition, and through that I got my first chance with you guys, and from here my career has just taken off.

Brian Priestman said one of the things to work out was just when to let go of the orchestra, when not to get in the way. As a conductor you feel you should be controlling the orchestra all the time, but you have to trust the players. For some people this is not enough – they like the feeling of being in control. I'd love to have my own orchestra one day in the right sort of environment. I was always very cautious about a kapellmeister's job - you can end up churning out things that you really don't want to conduct. The whole thing about my appointment in Graz is that I get to do my own productions and I can say no if there is something I really don't want to conduct, and they seem to be very happy with the whole arrangement.

The psychology between a conductor and orchestra is hard to define; it depends on the people concerned. People have conducting master classes given by other conductors but I think they could also be run by players. That's the other thing I enjoyed about my studies in America. One of my colleagues was a violinist and a percussionist and I learned as much from him because he had been playing professionally. When I was with Glyndebourne I would go and talk to the players in the pit and watch them work as an ensemble. Sometimes colleges and institutions forget that there is this huge resource of information within an orchestra. You may get five different views from the players but generally the information will be heading in the same direction. I think Simon Rattle said that he got really frustrated when he was at Bournemouth because he knew he wasn't bad enough for the orchestra to ignore him, but was good enough to get in the way. Working out when to and when not to interfere!

If I do ever get to a point where I want to stop conducting my next choice would be to train as a speech therapist as I've always been fascinated by the voice. In some ways I think it helps my conducting. Music is the most personal form of communication, from moving your bow to breathing and it all sort of comes from your gut which is where your singing comes from. I see this as being a help for me because I have never played in an orchestra though I did spend some time learning about string playing and I have played timpani and a bit of percussion. I had a composition teacher who said to me 'You can't write music until you've suffered a bit.' And I think the same for conducting too. Music goes down under so many different levels.

I don't know how I do what I do. If I'm with a large group of people I'm the last person who wants to talk. But stick me in front of 150 musicians and I'm quite happy to do my job. Some conductors stand in front of mirrors but I've never really understood what they learn by doing that. I don't know until I look at the people in front of me and the music begins what my arms are doing to do. It is weird. I have no firmly prescribed idea how a performance is going to go. Perhaps I'm a reactive conductor. I don't really know what is going to happen until I get what's coming at me from the other direction. I love watching the communication that goes on with the principals across the band, I think it's fascinating.

So I can't prescribe how to conduct something until I feel the sound or volume. I have my own ideas of how I would like it to go, but sometimes it's quite nice to open the channels in the other direction. There are times you need to say we are going to do this or that, but it is also quite fascinating to give the orchestra a chance to speak a bit themselves, in musical terms. You have 90 extremely talented players at your disposal and if they have an opportunity to express themselves and not switch off their own personalities, obviously it would make the experience so much better for them. Years ago the maestro was tops and the other day I overheard a conductor say to a student, 'It's not a democracy, it's a dictatorship!' There are moments when you have to make the decisions so that is true in some ways, but these days you have to be careful with that sort of attitude as it could turn the orchestra against you and that's generally not a good idea!'

GÜNTHER HERBIG

Günther was our principal guest conductor during Ted's reign at the helm, and was also very supportive during the BBC musicians' strike. He is on camera during the BBC 'Children in Need' charity day when, having finished a concert in Hanley, many of the orchestra drove back to headquarters and gave a performance of Rossini's 'William Tell Overture'. Easy enough, you think. However, the catch was that with BBC economies each instrument had to be played by two players. For the strings, one person bowed and the other held the instrument and fingered the notes. For the trombones, a second person used the slide. To our surprise and delight, Günther offered his services, unaware that the comedian Russ Abbot was in the studio and was concentrating so hard on what Günther was doing. Russ managed to mimic every action and suddenly we had two down beats to follow! On a more serious note, we performed a deeply rewarding and moving Bruckner 8 with Günther at the helm in 2009. Even as an octogenarian Günther had the whole work at his fingertips; such performances are engraved in one's mind forever. In April 1999, he explained his journey to the rostrum, through the turbulent times leading up to World War II.

'I can tell you about the situation in Germany and in America. First of all, you had to conclude your schooling at 18. Then you had to go through the examination for entry, and you had to have piano as your major instrument. For the first year, it was no conducting at all, just piano, and everything else that conductors had to study – theory, counterpoint, music history, but also pedagogy, psychology, philosophy. If you did not finish these five years of study and did not get your state exam you could not get a job. No-one could even invite you for an audition. So we had to have two years' lessons on one instrument of each family of orchestral instruments. So, as a child, I played piano, flute and the cello more or less at the same time. Piano was always my major. Then, in Hochschule, I had two years' percussion, two years' horn, and I continued playing the flute. We even had to have one year's

Günther Herbig. Photo by Tom Bangbala

singing lessons. Usually German conductors start in an opera house, you know, and it's very helpful if you know something about singing, even if you just learn that singers have to breathe. Some conductors don't know this!

Then, from second year on, we had conducting lessons and this was split, in my case. We had one professor for opera, and one for the symphonic repertoire. The one for the symphonic repertoire was Hermann Abendrot, one of the great German conductors (he was the Gewandhaus kapellmeister) and I studied three years with him. After five years you finish with the state exam and you try to get a job, which at that time was not difficult. I got a job at an opera house as a choral repetiteur. This is as you usually start. I worked my first year and at the end the music director who was to conduct the opera fell ill. I had played for all the rehearsals so I had to step in. It happened that the Interdant of a big opera house of the German Nationalist Theatre was in the audience because he wanted to hear a particular singer. He saw me and immediately offered me a job as kappellmeister, not of course the first position – this was the third. So I went there for five years conducting only opera, nothing else. Later I became music director in Potsdam conducting both opera and concerts.

Then I was offered, by Kurt Sanderling, the second position in the Berlin Symphony, where he was music director. I was there for four years, and was then offered the music director of the Dresden Philharmonic, which is already one of the big positions in Germany. Sanderling had always said that when he retired I could be his successor. I was always joking that he would never retire, but eventually he did, and I was offered the job in Berlin as music director! So I went back to Berlin for seven years. When I ran into such political trouble with 'The Party' I left and went to America. What I am trying to say is that it is a very long and thorough time of study that is required and a very gradual step up, one after the other. Young conductors today think, 'I will win one of the big conducting competitions, and then an international agency will take me and so on.'

Now in the United States there was always one or more young conductors sitting in the audience, listening to the rehearsals. They would come up to me and say, 'What advice can

111

you give me?' I found out that there is no strict system of educating conductors. So you can go one day here and the next day there; I found people who had studied one year at the conducting class at the university and then they went for the summer to Tanglewood. Having spent two weeks at the rehearsals of Bernstein they would declare that they were conductors and were very surprised that they did not succeed!

Now a very difficult thing for young composers in the States is when one looks for staff conductors. I always got between 185-220 applications for these jobs. You cannot have 200 people in front of the orchestra. So you had to make a decision and choose 20-25 as a maximum excluding at least 150 people. How do you do it? You may be very unjust. You go off the biography and where they have studied, recommendations they have - but this is not a serious guide. There is no other way, you know. So I know young conductors who are not young any more because after twenty years they have never had the chance to go and stand in front of an orchestra to audition. They were never invited!'

But we seem to have a shortage of conductors here – obviously not so in America?
'Well, the question is how good are they? They are self-declared conductors, you know. We tried to eliminate people after a discussion, before they came in contact with the orchestra. There was one young man, maybe 30-32, and I asked him if he had conducted already. 'Yes, I have done quite a few concerts, even one last night when we played Beethoven's Pastoral Symphony.' 'Can you tell me how many flutes there are?' 'Yes, there are two.' 'How many horns?' 'There are four.' 'How many trombones then?' 'Three!' So he had not realised that there was a piccolo, only two horns and only two trombones. How much had he known the score, conducting a concert without knowing how many musicians he had in front of him? The problem in the United States is that there is not an official stamp that says that this man has gone through a very thorough and serious training. Anyone can come in and say, 'I am a conductor.'

I had to discuss this many times with the American Symphony League. They asked why all the music directors of their major orchestras were not American. I had to reply that it wasn't a lack of talent. 'It's just how to find it, how to develop it, and then how you lead it from your studies into the actual profession.' 'Would you devise us an ideal curriculum for a post-graduate additional study for conductors?' I said I could do this, because I myself had been through this for two years with Karajan. I sent them an outline of a two year programme. I didn't hear anything from them for about six months, and then suddenly, they called me to say they had the funding in place and I could go ahead and start the course. 'You are the director - it will be located at Yale University and there are two orchestras to work with!'

My idea was that the students just needed artistic guidelines and inspiration. I thought they could be exposed every second week to a major international conductor – that would be OK. I gave them two weeks of my time; they had one week with Maazel, one with Zubin Mehta and one with Kurt Sanderling. Five times they went to New York to meet Leinsdorf, who was happy to do it, but too old to travel. Bernstein had promised to come, but that was for the year that he died. So this was my wonderful programme!

As usual in the United States the funding stopped after two or three years and the whole thing fell apart. Americans don't understand that quality has something to do with slowly putting one brick on top of another. They think it's something like a firework: once it is up in the air and gone they lose interest, they turn away, there is no money and everything falls apart.

When I was in Berlin, the leading conductors of East Germany and myself realised that there seemed to be a problem from finishing your final exams and starting your first job. Getting the job was relatively easy - East Germany had 17 million people and 84 symphony orchestras so there were so many opportunities. But there were many promising young conductors in their first or second year who were not prepared for everything that was required of them. It's not only the conducting (you can be a very good musician) but if you make psychological mistakes with the orchestra, which is very easy thing to do, you lose the trust of the musicians and you get nervous and tense.

So we thought we should try to design something that

would take a group of six to eight conductors who already have their orchestras, or who are first kappellmeisters in an opera house, and meet with them three times a year for two to three days in a small city. We would hire the orchestra of this city, and have workshops with them conducting compositions that they were to conduct with their own orchestras next time and give them advice. It was difficult to schedule but possible only because we organised it well in advance. We also sat down with them, asking them what problems they were encountering. 'Where do you need help? Are things going well or do you feel insecure?'And thank God this system has survived the demise of East Germany and is now in place in the whole of Germany. The programme has even been extended to three or four years for each person. The conductors are provided with recordings of their work with the radio orchestra, so they can achieve a higher level just by seeing how an orchestra reacts to what they are doing. This is important! As long as you are in a school there are a number of people around to help you; you feel as though you are packed in cotton wool! Suddenly the door opens, you go out and find there is no-one to ask for practical and professional advice.'

So the funding is still there in place in Germany at the moment?
'Yes! But look, if you are a doctor, you study physics or chemistry – it's a longer training. It is difficult to see with a conductor where the professional aspect lies – anybody can stand there and an orchestra will play, you know. Another big problem that occurs all over the world – the conductors who really know about this profession don't teach. They don't have time! And the ones who have the time are the ones who are not good enough to have a full schedule as conductors. Some very, very good conductors – world famous, like Karajan - would have a three hour workshop in the afternoon whenever he was in Berlin. It was even in his contract. Summer courses are also very helpful, but young conductors cannot rely only on going for four weeks to Tanglewood, two weeks somewhere else, and then one big competition to another.

I never took part in any competition. First of all, we were not allowed to travel in East Germany though I don't think that hurt me. On the contrary, some of the Karajan competition winners didn't get so far and Mariss Yansons only came third, you know. So the workshop idea is good, but it should be longer than a week. Igor Markevitch made one for four weeks every summer, I think, in Monte Carlo. It was a very intensive schedule, and designed only for conductors who already had a position and were at the beginning of their careers. This was an eye-opener: too many conductors were taking part so that no-one really got advice – it became a kind of mass production. In workshops you can give advice, discuss the different aspects of a score and how you approach it in the first place. What conductors seem to do now is buy all the CDs of a particular work they want to study. They sit there and listen to it but don't understand it. You really have to look into the score, analyse it, and know what is there. Unfortunately there is a lack of seriousness, diligence and thoroughness nowadays.

I studied immediately after the war. I had no turntable, no recorder; I did not even own a radio. We could not buy scores because they weren't available. We had to go to the library of the Hochschule for music and we had to give it back in three or four weeks. Sometimes we had to share with other students. It was very, very different from what students can do today, but don't! Maybe, partly because for them now it is too easy and accessible! Most of the works of the major repertoire I had not heard before I studied them with the score. This was how it was eighty years ago! You may have heard a piece once performed by your local orchestra but without a radio or a recording. It is hard to imagine that now.

Overall, I think a conductor has to be well educated – I mean beyond music. Music is part of a much wider art in general, of philosophy and the whole spiritual world. If you are too narrow minded and just concentrated on beating one, two, three, four, then it is little wonder that performances would be lacking and somehow empty. If someone does not really understand what he is conducting, then it is a pain. For instance, if you are conducting Beethoven and you have no idea of the Age of Enlightenment, what the ideas were at that time, you will not fully understand a piece like the 9th Symphony. If you have no idea of Schopenauer and Nietzsche you are at a loss with Wagner. You can make the beautiful melodies but the inner understanding will be lacking. If you don't know anything about the philosophy of the end of the nineteenth century, then Mahler is an enigma. So it is necessary – otherwise, you really are just beating time, and anybody can do that!

Becoming a conductor is most challenging and interesting, because it is an obsolete profession, coming from a time with a more authoritarian situation and structure of society as a whole. Somebody was there who said what everybody had to do, and the others just did it, without question. Let's say, 130-150 years ago, I'm sure that the average professional quality and average education of musicians was much, much lower than it is today. There was somebody needed to give direction, and the group would follow. Today, we are in a much higher degree of a democratic society than we had years ago, and you now have a hundred people in front of you who are much higher educated in general, who don't automatically take orders if they don't feel that it is the right thing to do. The last bastion of regimental society today is the military, you know. People at the top give the orders and the others do immediately what has to be done without question. Of course, this is under the threat of losing your life, either in combat, or from your superiors.

So, conductors are executing in a field which was designed in a completely different social environment. To maintain the following of a group of one hundred widely educated musicians is very, very difficult. I don't have an answer for this. Of course, you need integrity as a human being, otherwise survival is not possible and that is a good thing. This is a question that is never addressed in books about conducting and about conductors. Have you found anything written down about this?'

No, but most books I have come across were written a while ago...
'...By people who still came out of the authoritarian mould of the profession. To find the very fine line between not being authoritarian but strong enough to lead is very difficult. In a certain way it is comparable to political leaders, that is democratic ones, of course. People don't follow you because you are at the

top. After four years, at the next election, you get the sack! You have to accept that you can never convince one hundred per cent of a large group, because people are too different in their opinions.'

PAAVO JÄRVI

Originally from Tallinn, Estonia, Paavo moved to New York and studied with Leonard Bernstein. He became musical director of Cincinnati Symphony Orchestra and Frankfurt Radio Symphony Orchestra; in 2004 the artistic leader of the Deutsche Kammerphilharmonie Bremen, championing the works of Estonian composers like Ärvo Part, and presently the music director of Orchestre de Paris. In 1999 it was the first time Paavo had come to the BBC Philharmonic; he was completely jet-lagged, but not only managed a strenuous three hour rehearsal, but also gave up most of his lunch time to talk to me!

'The problem with conducting is that no-one really knows how to teach someone to become a conductor. My theory is that the most successful conducting teachers have been the ones who have been able intuitively to spot a natural conductor. Then they will supply that person with as much technical and theoretical knowledge and as many practical hints as they can. Musin, for example, would say 'I never teach interpretation, because I can't teach anyone to be a musician, I can only teach them to beat in time.' That's why we're looking at someone like Panula, who goes to the sauna with all the guys and, after a couple of hours of just talking about anything, he picks out four people who he thinks will become conductors simply by the way they react, the way they think. The sauna isn't the only place to do it but it's a very Finnish way. Also, when one studies with Jorma Panula in Helsinki, one is assured that the teacher is going to find the student as much practical opportunity as possible. After they graduate from the academy and even during their stay there they will have small orchestras to work with.'

Student orchestras?
'No! Small professional ones! What I notice these days is that there are no students in the hall watching rehearsals. What better lesson could there be than watching me or some other conductor take the first rehearsal of something? Maybe I will conduct it so

badly – then this is already a great lesson for them! The first meeting with an orchestra is something special. No teacher can tell you this, it's only what you see and what you get out of it for yourself.

It's also a question of interpretation. I attended rehearsals of about 25 different conductors when I was a student and I got one idea from one person and another idea from someone else. I have changed a lot of these ideas now but at least I had something to think about at the beginning. There were many things that I didn't know about Shostakovitch 5 until I'd been to rehearsals taken by Kurt Sanderling.

Having been a percussionist has helped me to understand what it is like to play in an orchestra and that has helped me to communicate easier, I think. There are lots of famous instrumentalists who turn to conducting, they think that being a musician is enough but there is nothing worse than a technically great conductor who has nothing to say musically or a great musician who has no conducting technique.

I was very lucky because I was the third conductor in the family, and my brother is the fourth; my father and uncle were both role models. There are very few teachers, Musin did very well in Moscow and Otto Werner Mueller is at the Curtis Institute in Philadelphia and the Julliard School of New York. Conductors sometimes have an apprentice, or a protégé as they call them now, who travels with him, comes to the rehearsals, and can give little hints along the way. Panula picks out conductors from hearing them play and deciding that they might know nothing at the moment but they might have potential. Another applicant might know everything but not be chosen. My teacher at the Curtis was Max Rudolph who wrote the famous book 'The Grammar of Conducting.' He said 'What I teach here will not give you a career; once you have a career what I teach you now is going to make life easier. The only thing that is going to give you a career is your *personality*.' He was very practical about it. If you walk off a plane having had no sleep that night and you rely solely on your shining personality, then you are not going to get very far. You must have skill as well.

Learning to conduct is a lengthy process. You don't get in

to a conducting course until you are 25, and then it takes another five years. So you are 30 and still might not have any work for two years after that. Determination is fine, but it often comes with a degree of arrogance.

When you have finished your training there ought to a way to gain practical experience. That's why the Finnish or Nordic system is very good. There are about 15 small orchestras in Finland and they have to be conducted by somebody and young students are there to do it. All famous Finnish conductors have conducted in every single small place in Scandinavia. Badly, probably! But you are not going to get better unless you try, you make mistakes along the way – it's a very human process.

I think that every British orchestra should have not one but three assistants, or at least two! There would be a competitive spirit among them to get the attention of the chief conductor, and also the approval of the orchestra. For a maximum of two years for each group you would be providing a pool of people who are actively seeking opportunities. That's a healthy situation. As an assistant in the USA, unfortunately, you can end up doing pop concerts and children's concerts with a Mickey Mouse mask or a bear outfit. One of my colleague's picture appeared in the season's brochure conducting in a chicken outfit. I'm talking about giving assistants the chance to conduct serious concerts.'

NICHOLAS KRAEMER

Permanent guest conductor of the Manchester Camerata and principal guest conductor of the Music of the Baroque, Chicago. Nicholas approached conducting via the harpsichord, and has forged strong links with El Sistema, the music system in Venezuela. We had the following discussion during the Haydn anniversary celebrations in 2009.

'The quandary of how somebody gets started is something that I think is very, very tough. Conductors who really have confidence in their abilities form their own orchestra, like Simon Rattle did. If you are at college you can get your friends to play for you. So, rather than be thrown in at the deep end, that is a professional orchestra, or even *any* orchestra, the aspiring conductor should try conducting a string quartet which is much easier to organise and, with only four people playing, they are much more likely to be vocal about what they need rather than an orchestra just sitting there and quietly thinking 'Shouldn't he be doing it like this?'
I think that would be a fantastic way of learning.

They used that approach on the 'Maestro' programme, didn't they?
'That's right! I hadn't remembered that. I've taught very informally and once famously on the television programme about seven years ago called 'Faking it!' I was teaching this guy who was a punk singer, so it was a bit of a joke, and he was put up against other 'real' conductors. It was a competition that he was supposed to win, but unfortunately he lost! (Laughing loudly.) This poor guy had to conduct the RPO who knew immediately who the faker was, but that didn't matter, because there were three judges - a critic, a violinist, and another instrumentalist. The critic thought my guy was the best! Very, very funny!
The whole thing about conducting is just knowing your music so very well, much better than your players. You have to be so far ahead of them. I don't mean you have to pick out all the

wrong notes – that's important, but everyone can hear the wrong notes if they're audible. So that isn't essential. There are famous stories of Boulez being able to hear the sixth horn. I think he could, in fact I think he still can!'

I was invited to play mandolin for a CD of Stravinsky's 'Le Rossignol', with Pierre Boulez conducting the BBC Symphony Orchestra, unfortunately missing a subtle key change in the middle of one of my solos. Of course, he spotted it straightaway!
'Do you do a lot on mandolin then?'

Mahler's 'Das Lied von der Erde' has come up quite a few times. It always seems a good idea to accept the job months ahead, until you realise you have to sit on the platform for an hour before you play anything. On a tour to Denmark I played violin for the first two movements and moved seats during the third, to be ready for the mandolin entry in the fourth. The instrument was not good enough to stay in tune for long, and there was no way of tuning it once the other movements were progressing. In one of the performances the plectrum fell off the stand as I was moving seats, landing precariously over a join in the wooden staging. Simon Rattle was conducting this piece in Liverpool many moons ago, and I was placed on a riser next to the bass clarinet, only to be told 'Mandolin, you are too loud!' Other solos include Shreker's 'Das Geburtstag der Infantin'– a rather sweet fairy tale and Respighi's 'Feste Romane'. At least I now have a more modern instrument, so it does stay in tune for longer!
  Moving away from fretwork, I was going to ask you about your connection with 'El Sistema' and the Simon Bolivar Youth Orchestra. How far have you got with the chamber music project?
'Not very far at all! I offered to put this together and they jumped at it. Abreu was very excited and said he was going to get five string quartets together and we would make a chamber orchestra. That would be the start.'

If he can't do it, then nobody can!
'Quite! But the thing is that he never works ahead. When you go, you have the most amazing time, and I think it *will* happen. At

124

some point I have to say 'It's now or never!' or I'll have to specify the dates we are coming and going. There are two orchestras there - 'A' is the first generation and 'B' the second. All the first generation players are now teachers or play in the opera orchestra.'

There must be the money available for them to become teachers then.
'Yes! What they want to do is to keep the players in Venezuela and pass on the system to the next generation. So the teachers carry on playing in the first generation orchestra and Simon Rattle worked with them while I worked with the younger ones. We put on a concert which was such a fantastic success they said 'You must come back!' It is wonderful when you go there, because there is *such* a response from the kids. When they were performing in London you could not get a ticket and in the foyer of the Festival Hall there were a thousand people watching a screen. The atmosphere was just fantastic – everybody cheering all the way through just like at a football match! Talk about crossing the line!'

So why is it not happening in this country then?
'But it is happening very slowly. You'd have to change the whole school system in Britain. In Venezuela they go to school from seven till twelve, and then they go to music school from two till six. Now what they are doing in Stirling is, I think, just that. I'm not absolutely sure of the timetable but it has to be every day. It's no good saying you're going to hold one session at the weekend, because you would get a terrific drop out - people going away for weekends or doing other things etc. This is just like school, but then it becomes not like school because you are doing something different, meeting people. Of course, to the Venezuelans, it is a way of existing.'

They probably don't have all the video games we have here.
'Well they have got all those, or some of them, at least. They are not all poor children though I know a lot is made of that point. In Britain we have three scholarships - Liverpool, Norwich and Stirling. I think the Stirling one is the most successful at the moment, and Richard Holloway has very strong connections with

them back in Venezuela. Each project really depends on a charismatic person in charge, one who is good at organising things.'

Was Abreu a musician originally?
'He was trained as a musician to start with, but was minister for finance. You can tell he is a conductor; he taught Gustavo Dudamel, of course. When I was over there it was the 30th anniversary of Sistema's first concert. They had all the members who were still in Venezuela, an orchestra of three hundred, at which Gustavo conducted Tchaikovsky 4. This is a sort of signature tune for Venezuela. The noise that came out of there was unbelievable! Nineteen double basses! And then Gustavo got Abreu to conduct the last movement again, which he has never done before. He hadn't conducted for at least twenty years, but of course they were all eating out of his hand.'

SIR CHARLES MACKERRAS CBE

Sir Charles Mackerras CBE. Photo by Tom Bangbala

Associated with the Sydney Symphony Orchestra 1982-85; the Welsh National Opera 1987-92; principal guest conductor of the Czech Philharmonic Orchestra 1997-2003.

Notable for promoting works of Janacek and performance of 18th and 19th century works as well as conducting 33 operas at Covent Garden. He is also the president of Trinity College of Music. These questions were put to him in between rehearsals for the Prom season in 2009.

Am I right in thinking that you gave a speech to the audience in Czech for our performances in the Prague Spring Festival one year?
'Oh yes I did! I can speak Czech and I do address all the Czech orchestras when I go there. They cease to be surprised any more! A lot of musicians, especially singers, have learned this minority

language because of Janacek. His operas have become very popular and it has become a sort of tradition to sing them in the original language which is quite difficult to pronounce. I get along with all these orchestras by speaking Czech. I studied there of course. I had learnt some German from Wagner operas (of course nobody actually speaks like that everyday) but then I found that one must not speak German in Prague because it reminds them of the occupation, and that was very recent, in 1947. In that time, 1947/48, I went on a British Council scholarship to study conducting. I got to know the operas of Janacek and they made a tremendous impression on me.'

You are known as a champion of Czech music, giving the first performance of a Janacek opera in the UK.
'Well, at first I didn't know Martinu. You see, just after the war, they were playing only Czech music. They didn't like German music, even Beethoven, who would have been horrified by the Nazis, and naturally they did play Mozart. There is a theatre there where 'Don Giovanni' was first performed, and that was still in the same state as it had been during the war. Of course, later it was renovated into a really proper theatre. I conducted this opera there, the first year after the communists had been thrown out in Prague, and it was really very good. It was a great occasion. Everyone was rejoicing that the communism was over. It was a marvellous feeling to think that we were working in the theatre where Mozart had worked. And when I studied there Vaclav Talich, who was the person I was really hoping to study with, had founded his Czech chamber orchestra, which he worked with very thoroughly - all young players but good ones. He had lots and lots of rehearsals, a huge number, and I used to go to these rehearsals and copy everything down that he said, because, although I tried to ask him to study with me he really didn't have time as he was also general musical director of the National Theatre.

Any rate, in Feb 1948, the communists took over and V. Talich was lucky to be ill with a cataract in his eyes. He was living very quietly in his villa outside Prague; otherwise he might well have been had up for apparent collaboration with the Germans because anyone who kept working during the occupation was later accused of collaborating. What could he do? He was MD of this huge opera house so in order to save the jobs of all those people he continued working there in the opera .Well, his misfortune was in a way my good fortune because I was able to go out to visit him and study scores with him. He had given the world premiere of Janacek's 'Sinfonietta' and a lovely production of 'Katya Kabanova'. That has since become a great favourite of mine and was the first Janacek opera I ever saw; it really made a tremendous impression on me because it is such strange music if you don't know it. Now everyone is familiar with it and if I am remembered for anything it will be for having literally introduced Janacek operas to this country. I came back with a vocal score of 'Katya' and while I was working at Sadlers Wells, the director, Norman Tucker, became very interested so they put it on there.'

This was the first performance of a Janacek opera in the UK in 1964?

'Yes it was! In Prague I studied in a class at the academy with a quite good conductor and I was able to study 'Rusalka', which is of course the most heavenly music by Smetana, along with the six tone poems. We also studied the 'Bartered Bride', which of course has these recitatives, not with piano but with strings, and you have to be a bit of a conductor to conduct those. They are very difficult! So that was my study in the academy. I didn't really know Martinu's music until somewhat later, because he was already living in America and considering returning to Czechoslovakia. An extraordinary thing happened - he wrote a letter to an acquaintance: 'Shall I accept this position of director at the conservatorium, what do you think?' And this person, who was actually in the government and was supposed to be a staunch communist, wrote back to him and said '*Don't on any account come here!*'

When Martinu died the communists asked to have all the memorabilia so they could place it in Policka, where he had been born, and there was this letter! It was lucky that the man had already died, otherwise he would have been in *terrible* trouble. Anyway I did get to know Martinu's music and did record a lot of it, still in communist time and with various orchestras and, as

129

German was not acceptable to be spoken, I did really have to learn Czech to get on there at all. As I was married by that time my wife also had to learn the language but for different reasons. She was constantly going shopping and there were terrible shortages after the war in Czechoslovakia.'

Did you think before you went there that you would have to learn Czech?
'Oh yes! We started to learn it at the Berlitz school a couple of weeks before we went, and we didn't get very far with it! It's a Slavonic language and has terrible complications in it. It has cases, you know - by, with, from, etc.- that all need different endings, but the worst thing in Slavonic languages is this question of *aspects of the verbs.* You use a different word whether you mean 'all the time' or 'only once' and it's almost impossible to get right.'

The short list for music director at Covent Garden in 1971 consisted of three names: yours, Ted's and Colin Davis's?
'Now you'll read in The Sunday Times what Ted said about the MD of Covent Garden. The interviewer asked all those years ago 'Were you very disappointed not to get the job of MD at Covent Garden when Solti retired?' He said, and this is the truth, 'There were three people being considered, Colin Davis, Charles Mackerras, and myself, and they chose Colin Davis.' They appointed him but we both got on very well with Colin and we continued to conduct as guests at Covent Garden. And in my case that was perfectly true. At that time I was MD at English National Opera at the Coliseum. I frequently would go one way to the Coliseum in the morning, and the other way to Covent Garden in the afternoon. There was one famous occasion when I conducted 'Il Trovatore' four times in one week – twice at Covent Garden, once on tour in Liverpool with the ENO in English, and once in the Paris Opera.

I would like to have become MD at Covent Garden, but my relations to the Garden have always been excellent; I've conducted a huge number of operas there. I do have a list of them somewhere!'

Your paths crossed with Ted's in Sydney as well - you conducting the opening Royal public concert at Sydney Opera House with 'Magic Flute', and Ted doing the first performance in the Opera House - Prokofiev's 'War and Peace'.

'At the first royal performance in the Sydney Opera House all the cast lined up, in order of appearance, to be presented to the Queen and Prince Philip during the interval. For some reason, the royal party entered from a different angle and were introduced first to Papageno and the two Men at Arms (who had yet to appear in the opera) and ended up with the music director and conductor, Ted Downes and myself! Ted did the opening performance in the opera part of the opera house – you realise that it's a concert hall and an opera theatre. The opera theatre was very unsuccessful and has got to be changed. It has a terrible acoustic. Originally they were going to use the big concert hall to double as an opera house. During the building of the opera house opera overtook the concerts in audience popularity, so they decided that they would have to have a separate opera theatre from the concert hall. Unfortunately they used the theatre that had been intended as a theatre for musicals and light things, so the pit was never large enough. I did 'Meistersingers' with twelve first violins, down to six basses, which is slightly smaller than it should be. With 'War and Peace' they had to have fewer strings the more wind they had. It was sort of deafening. If the timpani played at the end of the second act of 'Katya' or 'Janufa' the players just had to block their ears. It was frightful. They are thinking of changing that now, but I don't think they probably have got the money. The concert hall is quite good. There has been a DVD of the opening concert that I conducted which was all Wagner, with Birgit Nielson as the soloist. So that was a very successful concert and nobody worried about the acoustics. It was only in the opera theatre that it was so terrible. Another silly thing! They did 'Tannhäuser', which I think Ted also conducted. It was one of the first operas along with the 'Magic Flute' and 'War and Peace'. The pilgrims are supposed to be heard in the distance, go across the stage and fade away in the distance. What happened was, because there was no wing space, all the pilgrims were there singing and it didn't sound in the distance at all! In fact they were being miked up because they expected it to sound distant. So when they went on stage it was softer and then they went off stage and it got louder. Not the intention of Wagner, or anyone else!'

Some conductors have a very clear beat and some are rather vague!
'Somehow it doesn't seem to matter! If you are the kind of conductor who has a vague beat, you somehow still show what you want. A great example is Gergiev, yet everyone plays together and according to his wishes. He never rehearses, but somehow a very good interpretation is achieved, and the LSO all like him. So clarity of beat is important but it's not the only thing. Apart from Gergiev there was the famous example of the great Wilhelm Furtwängler who in my opinion was the greatest conductor who ever lived. He had a very unclear beat most of the time but not always. He was perfectly clear when he had to be but he expected the players to play behind the beat and in some way it worked beautifully, and the sound that was got out of the orchestra by Furtwängler was absolutely wonderful. The extraordinary thing that I still cannot explain after all my years of experience is *why* an orchestra sounds entirely different when the conductor is different. Some players say 'that is nonsense – it's the players who are playing,' but that is not true. There are conductors who like to rehearse a lot, some just say they are making their views clear about the work by their gestures and, of course, a very important thing is the training that conductors get in German opera houses where they have to walk into the pit *never* having worked with the exact personnel in the orchestra.'

Does that still happen these days?
'Oh yes! In Germany they still do it that way. The players change *all* the time.

The system finds you out as there are no rehearsals. You perform established productions while you rehearse the new ones. There are no regulations to insist that the same players do the rehearsal and the concert, so other players might be given the chance to play the first parts at the performance. You never know who is playing a familiar part and who is sight reading! It is really quite off-putting.

In Cologne you have a Hauptprobe and a general rehearsal. The Hauptprobe is the last time to run through the whole opera with a chance to rehearse a few details en route. The general rehearsal is the final run through with an audience present. Star players from the symphony orchestra could well come just for the general rehearsal.

They say that if you know your job as a conductor, then you have to cope with that sort of situation!

I don't have to tell you that many players, just on principle, have a go at the conductor, but the German orchestras, including the famous ones there, ones that I won't specify, are *extremely anti-conductor!* The funny thing is they say they don't like *any* conductor, and you say – what, not even one? And then they say, well maybe Carlos Kleiber, despite the fact that he was such an extraordinary fellow! He used to cancel all the time; he was so sort of moody - you never knew how he was going to take things. But they all worshipped him because he was such a wonderful conductor with beautiful gestures and everything; he made everyone *want* to play the music.'

What challenges lie in wait for conducting students at Trinity College of Music now that you are president?
'There is a conducting scholarship in my name, and this chap comes and watches me at rehearsals. The conductor of the ballet at Covent Garden took up the previous one on this scheme and had him conducting the 'Rite of Spring' which of course is a ballet and apparently he did it very well. Young conductors experimenting on you – it's rather a drag, isn't it? They don't know what to say, they beat the wrong thing, but they have got to practise somehow.'

You just don't want to be in the orchestra that they practise on, do you?
'It is difficult to train conductors except in technique so it's a question of how well the conductor knows the piece. Again, to quote that very unpredictable man Gergiev, he fiddles about but when he knows it's got to be together he becomes a very clear chap. I always thought he was a charlatan until I saw a film of him

giving a conducting class to young people in Holland with a work by Messiaen, which was frightfully complicated. He was talking to these students: 'Why do you make a fuss of that particular part? All you need to do is just go like that and they'll all play together.' I was amazed at how much he analysed that, I mean that was quite extraordinary. My respect for him went up quite a lot after that experience!

To watch Richard Strauss conducting was quite amusing. He conducted 'Till Eulenspiegel' as if he didn't like it! He was constantly licking his fingers and turning the pages, looking in the score all the time.'

Perhaps he didn't remember it very well?
'You know, often when composers have written something they can just forget all the details! Strauss was conducting the very difficult end of the second act of 'Rosenkavalier', that's the one with the waltz in it, which is very hard because of the changes of tempo, and he just looked bored when it was being played. But he would just give a flick of the wrist at the right time – and it all fell into place.'

Are there opportunities for conductors these days?
'Young conductors do get training in German opera houses in the way I've described. It's extraordinary how certain conductors just seem to have the flair and people engage with them. There are several extremely talented young conductors at the moment who, either through enthusiasm or whatever, seem to be quite successful.'

The future's looking good then?
'I think so. But the problem is - is the future of the whole classical music scene looking good? I'm not sure that is does! You see there is a terrible accusation all the time that classical music is snobbish, or elitist. These stupid words! And of course it is not! People have got it into their heads that it is, and how one can get rid of this concept I just don't know. All the time you can reach out to potential audiences, particularly the young people, but they just don't believe that classical music is not elitist and not what they

want to be in, unless they want to play it themselves. There is a very high standard of playing. It requires huge concentration to learn to play the violin, for instance. And all this time the pop music scene is taken so seriously and why should it be? I suppose because pop stars all seem to have political views and that's very trendy these days. It's a very noticeable thing that these days a person who is described as a musician is a *pop* musician and the type of musicians that we are have to be called *classical* musicians. I'm sure that classical music and orchestras are so important that they will go on, but I must say it is a struggle now. It would be terrible if they ever stopped subsidising BBC orchestras.'

JAMES MACMILLAN CBE

**H.K.Gruber and James Macmillan in the Green Room.
Photo by Andrew Price**

Appointed composer/ conductor of the BBC Phil. in 2000, having risen to fame with the premiere of 'The Confession of Isobel Gowdie' at the Proms in 1990, and the percussion concerto, 'Veni, Veni, Emmanuel', written for Evelyn Glennie, two years later. Here are some of his thoughts in 2009.

Simon Rattle says conductors ought to be composers. Would it help if composers were conductors, so they could understand what difficulties there are in performing some of the modern scores?
'Yes, it's cropped up quite a lot in discussion with composers that it would be very helpful for them to stand in front of a group of musicians in order for them to get their ideas across. I've seen that done on little courses. The composers stand up whether they want to or not and rehearse a piece of their own. I think it is important.

You find out practical things immediately not just about your own piece but general things - what instrumentalists have to do. It should be factored into their training as composers at university and college.'

You can write the same thing down on a page in different ways. Sometimes it's easy to pick up, and sometimes incredibly difficult.
'I've certainly noticed my writing changing, evolving, since I've had to do more conducting. The score of 'Confessions of Isobel Gowdie' has been done a lot but it is very tricky, much trickier than anything else I've written recently. I don't think it could have been written any other way, but I would be loathe to change some of those early pieces, even something that's nearly impossible. You need *concentration* especially when difficulties have to be conquered in an unfamiliar piece.'

You conduct many first performances of the works of young composers. This must be an area that interests you especially?
'Yes! I'm very much a supporter of my colleagues. I like not just the young composers but other living composers, the whole range of composers that we have done here over the last few years. I'm very much on their side. I've noticed that there is a whole range, a group of composers/conductors now, and that wasn't the case 20 or 30 years ago. Nowadays there's Thomas Ades, George Benjamin, Esa Pekka Salonen, Oliver Knussen, John Adams... There had been a separation of the two crafts, two specialisms. It's almost as if there is now a move back to the days of Wagner and Mahler, when conductors were composers and vice versa. There is something to be said about a composer's insight into another composer's music that I felt through having my work performed by people like Esa Pekka Salonen. They've got this composer's ear or eye. It's just not about a composer's solidarity it's something else, an unspoken, mysterious thing about the creative urge that composers kind of recognise. It's not the only way to do contemporary music - to have a composer/ conductor. Some of the best performances that I've heard were from people who weren't composers, so I can vouch for that, but there is something about the composer's instinct that is quite valuable to be thrown into the

mix.'

Can you learn from what these students write – what looks effective down on the page, but cause many problems for the musicians in trying to perform well? I'm thinking of constant time or key changes among other things.

'I've made a special study of a couple of pieces because I was intrigued with what the students were doing and I thought they had a real gift for colour or something. There are some works by these young composers that have impressed me some way, enough to make me revisit the scores weeks after the performance. On the other hand, one of the scores recently seemed to defeat me absolutely. I had nightmares about it even before getting here. I even changed something slightly and it didn't really help much. It's not often that I'm completely defeated and I really felt frustrated! I'm sure somebody would get it absolutely right if they had a much more mathematical brain. I just got flustered when I saw all those metric modulations coming up with a 5/32 bar right in the middle. It did make sense but actually when I changed that particular bar the composer himself didn't notice! That also teaches me a lesson - that certain things aren't worth doing even if they tend to impress other composers, because they look quite brainy on the page, but in practical terms the ideas are not good.'

It is often said that composers are too involved with their own music to be able to conduct their own works, but this does not seem to be a problem for you.

'I can understand the instinct to keep things separate. Musicians get used to people sometimes as composers and when they see you becoming a conductor they get a little perturbed. In other places, like Scotland when I started doing it, I don't think the people I worked with liked it, because they knew me one particular way. Ever since then, whenever I go, I've been known as a composer/conductor. There is a mindset sometimes that gets used to your doing one thing or another, if you're not careful.'

When Sir Peter Maxwell Davies comes here to conduct his own music he does seem to get a little too involved and become a tad over indulgent!

'I've noticed on some of Max's recordings he takes things much slower than he has marked. There is something about trying to disassociate yourself from the anxiety of hearing something in preparation. You can get awfully anxious about things not working and that affects your attitude to preparing a rehearsal. You shouldn't be anxious; you should pinpoint in a calculated way what is going wrong and sort it out and not get flustered. I just feel over the years that the way to do it, to make it all right, is to take the ego, the composer part, out of the equation. You have to be a technician! The music needs to be technically sorted out. So you do learn the hard way – or at least you should!'

John Casken was a mentor of yours and we premiered his first symphony 'Broken Consort' at the Proms in 2004. I thought the idea of a gypsy band made up of an electric violin, mandolin, accordion and cimbalom, all taken from members of the orchestra reacting with and against our colleagues in the full orchestra was a fascinating concept. As principal guest conductor of the Netherlands Radio Chamber Orchestra from 2010, what sort of repertoire would you like to do there?

'We are talking about repertoire just now. I'm doing a lot of my own music, and some Dutch composers as well. They want me to mix the programmes a lot more. At the last concert I did some Shostakovitch and some Britten. I am quite keen to conduct those as they are two of my favourite composers. They want me to do some Haydn and some Beethoven as well, which is a bit of a specialism. There'll certainly be lots of concertos and so on for players I like working with. I'm keen to take British music when I go abroad, because they don't know it. The string players in Belgium and Germany hadn't played the 'Fantasia' of Vaughan Williams; they'd heard about it, that it's supposed to be good and when they get to play it they will absolutely love it. How can you get through your whole career without playing pieces like that? It's just such a huge divide even with countries so close. I did a concert in Karlsruhe a few years ago and every single piece was unknown both to the orchestra and the audience, one of the pieces being mine. They were just dumbfounded and thought it was going

140

to be impossible when they first saw it. Sibelius 3 had not been done by the orchestra for fifty years! Sibelius doesn't seem to be done in Germany, they don't seem to like it that much. I'll probably take the 'Enigma Variations' of Elgar to Holland as well, or the Tippett 'Fantasia Concertante on a Theme of Corelli'; it's a big string piece, it's very tricky!'

How did you make the leap from composer to conductor?
'Well, I've always conducted ever since I was a little boy – being thrown in front of a choir or a band or something. I've never had a lesson in my life. I've had a few consultations in the last ten years when it became apparent that I would be doing a lot of it. I was able to go along and sit in some of the classes of Martyn Brabbins which was very useful and Colin Davis provided a completely different type of consultation. So I've just sort of jumped in at the deep end. To sink or swim! The real disasters were about ten years ago now. It all depends if you like the musicians and they like you. You don't know that until you actually start conducting.'

Composers appear to be home based and conductors see home rarely. How will you cope with this scenario?
'Yes you're right! One of the reasons I think I started conducting was in fact to get out of the house a bit. It's a very solitary life being a composer and that's good. Obviously I'm someone who does enjoy working with my fellow musicians and I felt a little frustrated at times. So I do have a strange life - some of it is very, very quiet and solitary at home with my family. I wouldn't say the balance is half and half yet. It would be wrong to make it that way for me - weeks away from home, living in hotels and that sort of thing, doing the thing that conductors do. It does settle down when you go to places that you are comfortable with. So I don't have that kind of homesickness that I did at the beginning. How *real* conductors cope with that all the time, with a family at home, I don't know. In 2004 I was away about half the year and it didn't feel right. So I have cut it back to something nearer a third or a quarter of the year. It sounds a lot but to some musicians it isn't.'

Conductors are doing so much travelling these days, is it possible that they do not have the time to study scores sufficiently, especially performances of newly composed pieces?

'There are some conductors who don't give the time to study the score before they come to the rehearsal. This is unforgivable, it's bad manners. I have seen conductors prepare things very sloppily, regarding it as a chore. This doesn't seem right even though they might not like the music. You've really got to be well prepared, for your own reputation, I think, otherwise it communicates to the orchestra that the music is not worth doing – and the conductor then is saying that the music is rubbish. I'd hate that to happen.'

COLIN METTERS

Colin Metters is Professor of Conducting and Director of Conducting Studies at the Royal Academy of Music in London, a course he himself founded in 1983. Through his continued dedication and commitment, this is now recognised internationally as one of the foremost conductor training programmes. In addition to his on-going commitment to the Royal Academy, Colin Metters continues to travel worldwide giving seminars and master classes. The Academy programme boasts an impressive list of alumni including the musical directors of Opera North (Richard Farnes), Reykjavik Symphony Orchestra (Rumon Gamba), and English National Opera (Ed Gardner); principal conductors of Birmingham Royal Ballet (Paul Murphy) and BBC Scottish Symphony Orchestra (Ilan Volkov); and Ludovic Morlot and Mark Wigglesworth, whose international careers have spanned America, the Far East and Australia. In 2010 he told me:

'To paraphrase the Bard, "to teach or not to teach, that is the question". It is no secret that there are those, often well respected in their own field inside and outside music, who believe - and are vocal to that effect - that conducting cannot be taught. It is clear to me that there is a basic and simple misunderstanding on the part of the doubters. Of course it is not possible to create talent where it doesn't exist - either someone has talent or they don't. But, there is a technical foundation for a conductor's ability to influence how an orchestra plays. That there is a basis for control and influence is proven by the simple fact that orchestras know immediately when the conductor doesn't have it. This is evidenced not just by the inability to convey the musical intentions but in the causing of frustration and annoyance to players, bewildered and confused by meaningless gestures that lead to the inevitable "heads down and let's get through it" solution. It is, of course, not just the physical aspect we are dealing with here but the emotional, intellectual and psychological plus all other aspects of the human psyche that are involved in understanding the relationship between conductor and orchestra and which are therefore a serious and legitimate part of our study.

The mercurial qualities of someone with a natural gift or talent - call it what you will - cannot be overestimated in conducting any more than a prodigious talent in a violinist or pianist. However, all the great performing masters past and present studied technique and practised! It perhaps should be said, to be fair to aspiring young conductors, that however good their training, they will always have less access to their "chosen instrument" than young instrumentalists.

Conducting technique is not a matter of individual style or idiosyncrasy but is built on certain fundamental principles involving control of beat speed, control of the midpoint in the beat, the physical vocabulary for all forms of attack, articulation, the gestural vocabulary to influence sonority, colour, quality of sound, not to mention the means to control tempo, tempo changes, rubato and the whole physical language of musical communication. Even these do not scratch the surface of what I believe is intrinsic to the study of the art and language of conducting. Although it is not possible to bestow talent or a natural gift, the art and craft of conducting *can* be studied, analysed and subsequently taught. Young conductors with ability can be mentored, guided and helped to be fully professional in every way in front of the orchestra. It is ultimately about growth and development, the gaining of experience and an incremental process of learning and maturing both as a human being and as a musician.

For conductors this learning process goes on all through life. It is not simply the physical side of it that is under discussion, but how a conductor works with an orchestra, the psychology of the work when things are going well and when they are not; how to treat players and how to speak to them; the use and psychology of rehearsal time, and how to deal with these problems. With some justification orchestras will be critical of young conductors (and sometimes the not so young!) when they fall short on any of the above. Orchestras know very well when the relationship works and when it doesn't. What is not always so clear is actually *why* it does or doesn't work. This should also be the basis of our study - to give conductors a working knowledge of

144

what is involved, the foundation of a conducting technique that will enable them to convey their musical intentions to the orchestra with the least amount of frustration to the players in rehearsal and performance and to be fully professional in all aspects of their work.

However comprehensive and well structured a conducting programme may be, the actual experience on the rostrum can only be finally learnt and understood in that particular environment in front of the orchestra. Whilst this is essential for the young conductor it often proves very frustrating for the orchestra. Attachment schemes such as those run by the Hallé and Bournemouth orchestras are of huge significance and are to be applauded. They provide the opportunity for the conductor to explore all aspects of their craft, to gain that very special and elusive experience within a supportive and constructive environment. They also present the opportunity to discuss issues with players, receiving real "feedback" as opposed just to criticism which can so often be the case.

Regrettably these schemes are limited and conductors often find themselves having to enter competitions to gain experience and (they hope) "launch" their careers. This is a far from satisfactory route since competitions are not in their raison d'être designed to be true learning experiences except of a rather questionable quality. In many circumstances it is the competition itself that is more important than the young conductors. The PR and promotion is geared to getting a winner, and what happens to the conductor after the big night is often forgotten. Those that win are often then "launched" on to a conducting circuit without the grounding and experience necessary to be able to sustain the pressure or the expectations. This can be a tough time for the young and relatively inexperienced conductor, not to mention the orchestras who are hoping and expecting something more than they often get.

'Conducting' has been described as 'the most comprehensive musical responsibility anyone can undertake'. This is as opposed to 'being a conductor', which is a completely different discussion! However, we are indeed dealing here with responsibility - responsibility to the music, to the composer, to the orchestra and to the listener. At all levels of music making - from a school orchestra to a youth, amateur, semi-professional and professional one - I believe passionately that there is an obligation to mentor young conductors to fulfil all aspects of their art and craft and to give them the means to be fully professional musicians in every aspect of their work. If we, as teachers and educators, care about music and music making, this is not a responsibility we can ignore.'

GIANANDREA NOSEDA.

Chief conductor of the BBC Phil. since Sept.2002, music director of Teatro Regio in Turin and artistic director of the Stresa Festival. Obtained recognition for the Beethoven cycle that was the first free download from the BBC Radio 3 website.

The following conversation took place during a break in recording a CD of 'Italian Classics' in April 2009:

I believe you studied at the Guiseppe Verdi Conservatory in Milan, where forerunners were Puccini, Muti and Abbado but not Verdi apparently!
'Yes, that is true! Our biggest genius was not allowed to get in to our conservatorium in Milano! Incredible!'

Franco Ferrara was a strong influence in Milan as regards conductor training. Did you ever meet him?
'No, I didn't, unfortunately. He has probably been the greatest teacher we have had in Italy. He had this master class in Siena, at the Accademia Chigiana, and everybody studied with him - Abbado, Muti, Daniel Barenboim- really all the great conductors. For one or two summers they had been students of Franco Ferrara. He was an incredibly talented conductor with a sort of epilepsy. It happened to him a few times as he was conducting in a concert that he would have a fit. So he eventually decided that he was too ashamed to go in front of the audience and the orchestra and lose control because of his illness. So he decided from a certain point in his life to become only a teacher - a good younger conductors' trainer. He not only had perfect pitch but a perfect sense of what 'sound' means and how to get that sound from the orchestra. Unfortunately when I started my studies as a young conductor he had already died. But of course I studied with my Italian teacher, Donato Renzetti, who was probably one of the best pupils of Franco Ferrara so I got the information and the traditions from Ferrara directly from the hands of Donato Renzetti. So I know more or less what his method of teaching was. And of course I

147

Gianandrea Noseda. Photo by Tom Bangbala

came across Muti, one of the best pupils of Ferrara, when he asked me to take extra rehearsals of Shostakovitch 5 and Scriabin's First symphony with the young orchestra when he had only three days to prepare the programme with them.

The conservatory in Milan in my time, the late 70s and 80s, was probably the best in Italy. I know someone from the Santa Cecilia in Rome will say differently; they will say *theirs* is the best one! Milan, especially in the 60s, 70s and 80s, is regarded as being the *real* college for musicians, not only for conductors. Imagine! Maurizio Pollini was a student from this college, studying in Milan as a pupil of Carlo Vidusso, besides conductors like Abbado, Chailly, and Daniele Gatti. We also had many good composers who taught, like Castiglioni and Azio Corghi, so it was a very good environment.'

The composing course was ten years?
'Yes! Ten years for composers, ten years for piano, and three for conductors! I don't know what happens these days.'

Solfeggio was an important part of Muti's training; does this tradition still carry on?
'The solfeggio system is very interesting! Absolutely! I'm not sure about its efficiency and effectiveness. Players and conductors are just killed by the Italian solfeggio. You are able to say the notes quickly, but after that you are not able to play them! In a way it is good as a conductor, because from the organising point of view it is spectacular. Theoretically it is fantastic! In the real life, if you have to play, it doesn't help because it is an extra level that you have to think of.'

I think the Curwen/ Kodaly system where the tonic of the major key is always referred to as 'doh' rather than the Italian one calling middle C as 'doh' does help singers and instrumentalists to think within the context of the key. The chords are so well in tune this way as is the intonation of a melodic line. There is a concentrated effort to reintroduce this system, but it will not happen overnight.
'I've been lucky myself because I have always had a talent for

sight reading. I ask how you are trained in England, because you are all so brilliant in reading and playing. It comes from a tradition. In Italy, I could tell you all the names of the notes in a symphony but what would be the point of that? With my orchestras in Italy and Spain I try to get them to play and produce 'sound'. Not to 'read, translate, command and then play as happens with our solfeggio.'

Your liking for Dallapiccola, does it stem from the composition course in Milan?
'I did the course in 8 years rather than 10 as did my younger colleague Daniele Gatti. The point of view of a conductor is different from the point of view of a composer. You have to understand what the composer wants, but you have to translate in a very concrete and realistic way: that note goes there, he will take over the line from there, the reason why he put the lines like this is because it is connected, but it is not a worry for the orchestral players. Unless someone asks me specifically to do more then I am quite happy about it. You know in a three hour or six hour session we have to be very efficient. But having said that, what is very important is the last part of the composition course when you start to orchestrate. How to put a melody for an instrument into the texture: how high, how low, how will it sound on the oboe or with viola, or clarinet with viola; trombone with double bass, or trombone with viola. You then try to write pieces to describe these situations. I made many transcriptions of piano music for an orchestra to see what might or might not work. This is very good training because it develops your sense of hearing and listening. If you hear something wrong in the balance, or you want a different timbre – coping with this situation comes as a result of that part of the course.

But basically, I think, before you stand in front of the orchestra, you should imagine clearly the sound you want to get, because if you haven't any clear ideas, then it is difficult for you to make adjustments. If you say 'Let's try this 'and 'let's try that' it immediately gives the impression that you don't know what you want. You can say sometimes 'I don't know what I want to achieve, but let me try this', and you just play the game and show

150

your cards. 'Forgive me, I'm not good enough to imagine what I want here, so let's try this'. It's like being a cook. A chef knows very much how much pepper or whatever is necessary according to the recipe, but sometimes he has to experiment, to try a little more of this and much less of that!'

This is where the student conductors fall down.
'Yes! The students do not have the possibility, and there is no teacher who has the time to tell you these things. I've been lucky, because I could study ten days with Valery Gergiev in Siena, the same Accademica Chigiana that Franco Ferrara used for his the master class in 1993. The only thing he tried to pass on to the students was 'what kind of sound did you have in your mind?' 'Oh, I don't know!' might be the reply. 'So, step down from the podium. Think; use your imagination. When you are ready you come and tell me. You can have an idea that you don't know *how* to get but if you do not know what you are looking for...' That was incredible advice because he was opening the window; he was opening a completely different world. What is crucial when you go in front of the orchestra is to show you are looking for something precise. Even if you don't understand something from the orchestra, the strategy is to get to your destination. Clearly have an idea. That for me is important, because what I hate is *wasting time.* I think everybody hates to *waste time!*'

Being a protégé of Valery Gergiev, you seem to be following in his footsteps in jet- setting round the world, with concerts in different continents on successive days. How does one cope in the fast lane? Do you ever stop and have some time to relax and unwind at home?
'Ah! I try to imitate Valery in making music but not in the life style he's just living.'

But your life is pretty hectic too!
'Yes! But believe me, if you compare my life with Valery's life, I don't regret it but I'm *miles* away from him. He comes from the Caucasus, the high mountains of Southern Russia, so he has a very strong character and a huge stamina. His ancestors were warriors.

So he has the character of a warrior with endless energy. I have a lot of energy, of course, but if I would try to compare myself with Valery I would lose. I think I try to do many things, but I still try to find the time to rest, to lead a normal life, to go to buy food and cook, to read books, to spend time with my nephews, to be in communication with my parents, who I see so rarely. In this case you would not call me a very good son but, whenever I can, I try to keep the contact alive. From the professional point of view you can run all over the world like a globe-trotter, but there is a certain point when this travelling is dragging the life out of you, taking all your energy and your imagination. So when you go in front of the orchestra you are bored, you are annoyed, you are empty. This has happened to me a couple of times in the past two years and I think 'What for? Why I am doing that?'

It just amazes me that some conductors have connections to so many orchestras. How do they do it?
'When I started to conduct compared to now I travelled *less and* conducted more orchestras, because you have to spread yourself just to get yourself known. Now, I travel more, I'm busier, but I see fewer orchestras, so at least I can decide which orchestras I like to work with. Let's see- now I *can* say - 'If I *have* to go there I would rather stay at home and rest'. Having said that my main jobs are the BBC Philharmonic, the Opera House in Turin, and the Met. (It is difficult to say 'no' to the Met!) Now I just try to find ten days or two weeks off. My wife is blaming me because I don't succeed very well, but I try very hard.'

You have a liking for grand dramas like Liszt's 'Faust' and' Dante'; Prokofiev's 'Stone Flower'; Strauss's 'Salome'; Tchaikovsky's 'Queen of Spades'; Puccini's 'Il Tabarro'; Verdi's 'Requiem'; Haydn's 'Creation'. You've conducted all these here. Is this the Italian spirit coming out?
'I am convinced that not only an operatic atmosphere is connected with Italian souls but also the fact that we are very ...open. We speak loudly, we give kisses to people, even people we do not know very well, we just do. You can like or dislike it, but we are like that. We try to be (we say in Italian) 'Solare' – 'the sun

shining'- which is very positive. We go over the limit, I have to admit that. Being like this gives us, as Italians, very close connection with the dramas in the operas, you know: jealousy, drama, death, life; faithful and unfaithful people; big dramas like playing the games in the casino in the 'Queen of Spades'. So they are all the experiences in the way we live. I've never been in a casino but I imagine the story. I imagine how it goes there, with people betting, trying to get the money, the beautiful women, trying to get in contact with them; sometimes the imagination is even bigger than the real thing. This also gives us the possibility to believe in the plot of the opera; if we are detached or disconnected no-one in the audience will believe us. It is difficult to believe the plot sometimes. You have to be incredibly convincing, you have to believe very strongly what is going on in order to involve the orchestra and to involve the singers. If you achieve this you will have the audience behind you. The stories are not impossible but they do not occur in daily life. Of course the daily life would not interest the librettists or the composers - they are looking for something exceptional, something fantastic!'

What else interests you, apart from grand operas?
'Of course with operas, the list is endless because apart from Verdi, Wagner, Strauss, we have all the bel canto operas and then Britten and 'Peter Grimes'. In the beginning, I couldn't get very involved with British music. Forgive me if I say that! Having now done the 'Four Sea Interludes', 'Les Illuminations', and 'Enigma', there is something that is challenging me, attracting me. When that happens, it means that you are trying to get a little closer to the British culture. There is the wonderful piece 'Falstaff' of Elgar - very rarely done and at some point I want to do a V. Williams symphony. After coming here for seven years I do feel more connected to the British way of viewing life, which is very different from the Italian way. I'm not saying it is better or worse, it's just different. Despite the fact that I am open and noisy, I am learning to be more private and intimate. So you see, I'm adding one more string to my bow!'

Concert halls in Japan and China were wonderful; halls were full

153

and we received much applause from an enthusiastic audience.
What is the future for music in Britain?
'Britain is quite lucky compared to my country, but of course it's not as good as Japan and China. Classical music is still new there. What I'm trying to do in Italy and in the university here, is to take the chamber groups from our orchestra. I talk with the teachers not the student. The teachers are coming but not the students – I see very few. My idea was to get involved with the 18-25 year olds. The university population in Manchester is huge. So far I have not been very successful but I will insist and we'll see how it goes. I'm doing the same thing in Torino. I'm inviting the 8-18 years old to the Teatro to spend some time with them. I tell them about music, what is a theatre, why we still do opera, and why we still do classical music. That is the secret. Just to invest time, not only money, but time. When I was younger, the conductor was a meteoric figure. So there was God, then the conductor and the rest were human beings. That is *not* the rule of the conductor. The conductor is just a normal person doing a job; some can be more inspiring, some less so, but it is not because God gives you the intelligence. It calls for hard work and talent, so you must be thankful to your parents and to God. I am here and I need you to make music - I need *everybody* in the orchestra. I'm not a dictator, that is very far away from my character.'

How did Gustavo Dudamel and El Sistema become so successful when there are so few training courses for conductors today?
'Dudamel is something exceptional! He is not only the most talented young conductor that I have ever come across, but Jose Antonio Abreu - *he* was the one with the idea back in 1975! *This* is the man who deserves the medals. How you think about starting this programme, I don't know! It is fantastic because with that orchestra and that system, coming out from the favelas, 'Come in and join in, find an instrument and come and make music'. It is not a reality coming from money, the money is not coming from the aristocracy, from the noblesse, but it's coming from the street. The *idea* comes before the money. After that, you have to pass the idea on to other people. 'Do you want to help me?' 'Do you want to join me in this project?' A conductor has to start with a particular

154

sound in his mind whereas with Abreu you start with an *idea* in your mind. This guy had such a great idea:
'Help me!' 'Help me!' And just look at the result!'

LIBOR PESEK

Libor was born in Prague and studied conducting, piano, cello and trombone there. He was principal conductor of the Royal Liverpool Philharmonic Orchestra 1987-98 and then became conductor laureate. He is renowned for his interpretations of Czech music. He came to the BBC Phil. in Mar.1999 and shared his thoughts during a break in one of the rehearsals.

If someone came to you wanting to become a conductor what would you suggest?
'Knowledge of a stringed instrument is very important and I think the piano, in the sense of understanding the structure and harmony and everything. I don't think that it is necessary to have a wind instrument but it helps if you have ever played one in the sense that you breathe with them.'

We have just had a workshop for conductor: is that a good route to take?
'Experience is everything! The best thing I did was to form my own chamber ensemble. They were professionals and we made chamber music on a volunteer basis. Many professional musicians feel deprived of chamber music work and if you find such a group this is an excellent way of getting some conducting experience. This is how I started after my academic study.'

Do you think there is any way to improve the courses presently on offer?
'I think I am now at a stage in my life where I would like to transfer my experience to other colleagues. It would be more or less volunteer work. I think I owe a lot to the North West of England and I wish that someone would approach me and give me some sort of schedule – some plan. I would be really happy to do that.
There is a lot of natural psychology in the work that you get through the years and years of experience. Just consider the players as artists. I think the orchestra starts to play well when you

157

let them express themselves and not to stop them every three bars or so; this is very discouraging. The young conductors are prepared well, they know everything down to the last semiquaver, but they don't quite know how to put it over to the orchestra. The orchestra is a living ensemble which has its own rules, unwritten rules, and it takes years of experience to discover these. The audience are entitled to enjoy the music without feeling how difficult it is to produce it. They don't have to be able to read music – they regularly come to the concerts and hope to have an enjoyable experience.'

There are very few British conductors coming through the system. How do we improve on that?
'British conductors are welcomed abroad but at home the orchestras remember them as greenhorns. They have a better chance once they've spent some time abroad and return at a more mature level. Conductors in their early twenties think they know everything and try to tell everyone how things should happen. As you mellow you make more contact with the players and the orchestra start to play better for you. It's a mass psychology which transmits. You know how it is – you can see a self-centred man who is only interested in his own success, you try to play your best but you don't have that special relationship which is so necessary for those expressive big tunes etc.'

Yes! It's a really good feeling to be situated in the middle of the orchestra and be able to say to oneself, 'You know, I'm really enjoying this!'
'Absolutely! As I say it is a complex question and, I don't know, probably there will never be a time when society will give young conductors the opportunity to mature on real life orchestras. It costs money. On the other hand, the managers and public want names that have accomplished something.'

I think, in America, you graduate at the age of twenty-five, and then you start a five year conducting course.
'Absolutely! And they either make it or not, and if not then the guys from Europe come in and do the job for you. It is unfair, it

seems, but all of the orchestral players probably wanted to be soloists one day or planned to be soloists. It's a general question of life's philosophy, that you can't have everything. One has to be a bit modest, know one's limits and be well-balanced. Also not to get bitter. Bitterness in people is a very negative thing.'

Do you get a buzz from conducting a top rate orchestra and improving them a small amount, or a lower grade one and improving them a lot?
'Well! At my age you get to be a little impatient! There were times when I've formed at least three good to excellent chamber orchestras back in the Czech republic and I enjoyed that and I would say that I guided some orchestras both in the Czech republic and Liverpool to some degree of integration. When I came to Liverpool I found the orchestra to be very well prepared by Mr. Janovsky, but I had the feeling that he didn't like Liverpool very much and was slightly negligent about the orchestra. But I came with my love and I believe what really made the sound of Liverpool in the ten years was that I cared for them, and they liked the way I trusted them. Again 'psychology'; not that I was any better than Mr. Janovsky , on the contrary, but I cared more.'

That feeling came across when I came over to play mandolin in Prokofiev's 'Romeo and Juliet'.
'Yes, yes! So you remember that; it was quite a nice recording. I still have it.'

Pam: Ah! So do I !

Vassily Sinaisky. Photo by Tom Bangbala

VASSILY SINAISKY

Winner of the Karajan Competition in 1973, having studied with Ilya Musin. Chief guest conductor of the Phil. since 1996, and very popular with audiences everywhere. Conducted the Phil.on a tour to Beijing, performing in the Cube, and the Great Hall of the People on New Year's Eve 2008/9. This interview took place early in 2009.

Do you know that I have been here in Manchester for thirteen years?

Time goes quickly when you are enjoying yourself! You are always so enthusiastic – are you able to choose the concert programme?
'No. I am not. Sometimes we have discussions, to see how they could calculate all this. Mostly, I am given the ideas from the management, you see, with some corrections of course. I would say 'no' to modern pieces and composers!'

You know the scores inside out before the first rehearsal. What is the process for learning a new piece – studying the score first and then buying all the CDs you can? You are well known in the local music shop!
'No! I think the opposite. Firstly, of course, I look it through, if it's a new score for me. Then I listen with the score, maybe twice, with two different conductors. Then I put the CDs on the shelf and I begin to play the music through on the piano a few times. At this stage I'm in the middle of the process of learning - I know its construction, its shading. Usually my first impression is correct (if I like the recording). If I think the recording is boring I'll consider it and save my opinion till later.'

You've been working with the Malmo Philharmonic, the Yomiuri Nippon Symphony Orchestra, the Tokyo and Malaysian Philharmonic Orchestras to name just a few. Do different orchestras have a different feel to them?

161

'Malmo is said to have a cool, clear sound. Nowadays, orchestral sound is not so very different. Before the war the Vienna and the Berlin Philharmonic had a very different sound. Compare the recordings of Bruno Walter with those of Furtwängler. Now I can tell you that the quality of sound is *not* very different. For example, Malmo has quite a cool sound normally, but now with me they play a lot more expansively. The Yomiuri Nippon Symphony Orchestra is *extremely* emotional. It is all very strange! So we're not only talking about Europe, you see, but we have international players, very many foreigners in each orchestra, so there is not a very big difference in the sound they create.'

A bit like Premiership football teams, then?
'Yes, unfortunately! But I still think that British orchestras have something special, not maybe in the sound they produce but in good ensemble playing. They understand things quicker, they are more active and more sensitive to conductors. In contrast, there are many other orchestras where the players cannot concentrate for very long and are sitting there quite uninterested.'

I understand that British orchestras are the good sight readers!
'Yes, but not only that!'

You know the names of players, you encourage them in the concerts with eye contact, gestures etc. Was this an important feature of your training?
'For me I think Karajan's way was more formal. During the rehearsals he was very exact. I attended two of them in 1973. He watched everyone and used names of some of the musicians. And then he told them that at the concert he *must* be in his own world. I don't like that idea at all. If you see videos of, say, Bruno Walter, you see him looking at the first clarinet or trumpet, or even a group of players. I *do* like that!'

You do need encouragement if you are going to play a solo.
'And if a conductor conducts just for himself he is out of touch, so you as a player play for yourself. I think it's the wrong way! For many conductors they find it easier to concentrate maybe, I don't

know! For me, I always feel that the live sound comes to me and I can create an ideal with that. I can do more or less something here. I'm very, very happy if the sound is even better than I can imagine. I think that the eye contact is even more important than the gesture.'

Ilya Musin must have been a revered conductor trainer. How did he choose his pupils?
'He chose to work with only a few people. People would come to his class before exam time. Sometimes he recommended them, sometimes he wasn't so keen, and so they had to move to another class. He was such a great name that the best wanted to go to him - that was to be expected.'

Winning the gold medal at the Karajan Competition in 1973 was a great achievement, but did it help further your career?
'It didn't help too much, except for the first two or three years when it was pushed by some of my managers because I was *SOVIET*. There was a terrible organisation called GOS Concert, who controlled everything and you couldn't do anything! Orchestras would just invite me and then the process developed from that. Sometimes people objected to Karajan; he was an official figure and not everybody liked him. Some related the organisation around Karajan to the mafia. So it was sometimes difficult to get bookings from any orchestra.'

Even knowing the score as well as you do, you are always trying to balance the melodic lines. One day we'll write 'f' in the parts, the next day this might be too strong and we change it to something lighter. Is this because you are turning the music over in your mind overnight and coming back the next day with fresh ideas?
'I can tell you that sometimes, when you reach this level of playing, suddenly someone in the woodwinds for example plays more emotionally. In this case, if the first violins are answering him or her, you have to instruct them to be more emotional too. So it's never 100% certain. Besides, I like some improvisation as well in the concert. I can tell you that as a player and a musician if you conduct and have too much control it narrows down the

possibilities in musical life. And of course I know now that the conditions and acoustics of the Bridgewater Hall and our studio in Manchester are different, and I adjust here because I know what it will be like when we get to the Bridgewater.'

To get a special effect, you ask for bowings to be altered, yet you give us hardly any time to write them in all the parts. Is this because you are always in a rush to make the most out of a rehearsal and keep everyone occupied for as long as possible?
'I can tell you that I think more and more that it is a very good system for all conductors to bring their own music with all their bowings and comments written in. It would make life so much easier. But I am a little bit lazy! You remember the Tchaikovsky 4 we did recently? Those were my own parts - I asked the librarian in Malmo if he would obtain that edition for me. When your material here is different you have to wait for the strings to put in bowings and you lose the concentration of the woodwinds and brass players. If you ask the two clarinets to play 'pianissimo' instead of 'piano', they would have done this anyway if it had been in their parts. So if the material had been prepared you could then concentrate on so many other things. There are some conductors who still do this.'

If you have a big repertoire you cannot do it, of course.
'In classical symphonies it is much easier, but in a large hall you want to change articulations and balance because it is not only emotions that you are concerned with.'

It's likely that the next conductor will come along and change it all...
'...and the one after that will want different things again. In big orchestras in America they have several versions of the same material. They can mark one set of parts and then put them away for another time, so when another conductor comes along they can start again!'
You seem to have a wardrobe full of gestures to describe the changing emotions of the music. Are these inspirational at the time?

'Yes! Sometimes you can feel differently in that part of the symphony. You have to find some special words for occasions like that, because words and music are sometimes saying opposite things. Sometimes, as a conductor, you have to give the musicians some ideas. I think now the conductor could be free to use his imagination. My position is that you are all good musicians, you know a lot about the background to the music, much more so than players did before World War II. I know now I just have to give sometimes a small idea. For example, today I asked the brass to imagine Mont Blanc. I had not prepared this statement - I suddenly thought this passage would convey something like a big mountain. So sometimes I improvise, I think about the character and I try to find a word to describe it. I think it makes it more interesting for you if I explain what the composer wants here rather than saying louder or softer etc. That is boring, so why not use the imagination instead! But it does have an opposite side. You cannot just rely on imagination. A conductor should have a good balance between technical things and imaginative ones.'

Conducting is a lonely life. It must be an advantage having your wife travel round with you. Does she help in the research you obviously do or does she have her own interests?
'I personally know my wife from my school days, we were in the same class. I met her when I was fourteen years old, so together we are like one body. She has listened to the CDs, she is a very good pianist and I respect her advice. At the same time she is always a little bit shy and I have to encourage her to tell me what she is thinking.'

After such a superb, intense Russian training, what is the hope of anyone in training at the present or, for that matter, in the future? Will we have the one rehearsal, one concert approach that Mravinsky hated?
'I shall be happy if the next generation of conductors are on the more professional side. Conductors many years ago were considered to be at the top of the music profession, but now many are half professional, half amateurs. You could be a very good musician and no conductor. So I'll be happy if there are fewer

conductors but of a higher quality. You have to know more about the piece of music than the player, who is now a high level musician. You need to know about the composer, his private life etc.; you have to be very communicative if your technique is very limited. It's also a great tragedy for the musicians, because they want to understand. On the other side, you know how many conductors now just have a clear beat and nothing else. What is a beat in music? What does it convey? You see nothing as a musician for you to interpret. Nothing more, nothing less!'

And if the length of training gets shortened due to financial problems?
'I don't think the length of training comes into it, either three years or five. You have to find a good teacher, but I can tell you that Professor Musin stopped with me to develop my technique after two years. He told me that I was a professional by then, but we discussed musical things for many years afterwards, about five or six years in fact, about different composers and so on and so on. Teaching conducting is a very individual process. For example, I recently came across a student conducting who couldn't give a good up-beat, but you could see that his body, his fingers, were so naturally musical. Then next day a cellist came, he was for twenty years a principal cellist of an orchestra. We played the Tchaikovsky Serenade (singing the theme of the waltz lyrically) and he conducted a strong, forceful, rigid one-in-a-bar. Brumm, brumm, brumm! I cried out 'But try to do *LEGATO*!''

I believe Jorma Panula takes his pupils into the sauna to discuss musical things.
'He is a good conductor trainer, but getting a little old now. I know the remarks he made for his Sibelius' symphonies are very professional, like 'bring out the clarinet a little more here'. Musin was more universal, perhaps? For example, he trained Gergiev; he did not give him his style of conducting but his understanding of the music. Many people feel now, if they get only technique that is enough for conducting.'

That was exactly the problem in our workshop; the personality of

166

the young conductors just did not come through.

'Musin has trained more than eighty conductors. Yes, eighty conductors! Some of the professors now are pupils of Musin but not the very best! I think you must be a good conductor first and have a good practical knowledge to be able to advise others well. Sometimes they are asked how to conduct a clarinet with the strings, but they do not know how to combine them. I know, but they don't! I think that situation is not very good. And it is similar in Moscow.'

So what's going to happen to the orchestral world in the future?
'For orchestras there is not a very good future, especially for the smaller ones! In America the future is quite good as we usually play the same concert three or four times! Even so they still have problems and crises and so on. Japan is good, Australia is good, in Europe not so good, even in Germany! Even in Berlin there is now no chance to play the same concert three times. So, for the future, I just don't know!'

Vassily Sinaisky and Nigel Jay on the Great Wall of China.
Photo by Andrew Price

Yan Pascal Tortelier and Jean Yves Thibaubet.
Photo by Tom Bangbala

YAN PASCAL TORTELIER

Principal conductor of the BBC Phil. from 1992-2003 when he was awarded the title of conductor laureate. Became principal guest conductor of the Pittsburgh and the São Paulo Symphony Orchestra. He also has close associations with the National Youth Orchestra. It is obvious to everyone coming into contact with Pascal that he is passionately involved with all aspects of music making. No half measures, sometimes over the top, but loved by audiences and players alike, that 'je ne sais quoi' feeling shining through. He is very fond of the eccentricities of Berlioz and has been highly praised for his orchestration of Ravel's 'Piano Trio', premiered in 1992. How many times would he quiz various players to get their opinion on subtle changes he was making to the orchestral parts for them to discover a few months later that he had changed his mind and thought of something fresh! He would get frustrated quickly if he could not achieve the sounds that he wanted, but would show obvious delight when something special happened in the performances. Pascal was one of the mentors for the programme in 1998 called 'I want to be a conductor' and our discussion followed soon after.

With the workshop we did here the orchestra hoped the standard was going to be quite a bit higher. The orchestras can't survive if there are no conductors coming up in the ranks, so is there any other way of training them?

'No! Of course it is a matter of training, but you cannot expect to see so many conductors around because, by definition, you get one conductor for ninety players. The rule is that the conductor has something special to offer to an orchestra, and it has to be within himself, and it has to be developed through studies, very long and deep and bold studies through playing, of course. It's not just about theoretical studies, but it is all a gradual process and you would not expect too many people to have that ability too soon, or to have the capability to become a proper conductor. So, I understand your point that you were disappointed with the level shown here, but let me make the point that if we can pick one talented conductor out of, say, a dozen, you would not expect more because otherwise the profession would be crowded with conductors – you would have more conductors than players! It doesn't quite work that way. Well, I suppose it's crowded with lots of people who would like to do it.

There are so many elements and components in a conductor's activity and life that it is far from being the easy job that one might figure. You know, honestly, in my early days when I was leading an orchestra I never suspected that it would be so demanding and that it would take me twenty years to establish myself, not just to establish a career, but as a musician, as a conductor. Just to get the experience, the knowledge, the poise, the assurance, the confidence to do it. It's taken twenty years to become, hopefully, a decent conductor, on top of my twenty years' studies as a musician altogether, so what do you expect? You cannot see talented conductors coming just like that, out of the blue! It's a long process!'

Do you think the conservatoires could help? The students never get in front of a professional orchestra.
'I really think that could be the case in a number of schools. The Royal Northern College of Music has a special scheme for conductors where they spend two years studying. They pick two conductors each year and I think that's about right to limit their scheme like that.

The dilemma is this: on the one hand, you are telling me, how can we offer a young conductor the chance to develop and experience conducting with a professional orchestra like ours, but on the other hand, when we have a conductor who has very little experience, an orchestra like this one is saying 'Well, this is not what we are here for! We are not here to train youngsters!' And you are telling me – could we train youngsters? So how do we balance it, that is the problem!'

But if we don't get some sort of balance, there aren't going to be any conductors or many orchestras in the foreseeable future.
'I think you are being very pessimistic or negative even. Is it a statement you are making to me that the level of conducting has

gone down?'

No! I just wonder if there are so many conducting competitions these days. This workshop idea has been described as the best thing since sliced bread!

'Sliced bread...I like that! But I think when the time comes, perhaps a new assistant conductor will be recruited in a similar way to this in the future. I think it's the best we can do. We gave a chance to twelve youngsters which is not always the case, because if you take most of the orchestras in the world they will audition about thirty conductors but not give them a chance to attend a week's workshop! I know a week is not very long, but better to develop some sort of contact than just one audition in front of a panel. In our scheme there was a nice feeling of collaboration and exchange in talking. It was very friendly, I thought, and for a number of them I think it has been very critical when they realised 'Oh, my God! Conducting is not what I thought it was going to be!'

I understand how they felt because I remember in my early days (until not so long ago) there were moments when I felt just the same as they did. That is to say, the moment of sheer inner panic you are trying to control which, of course, you should never show to the orchestra. This panic, where you think you're not making it - it's the most extraordinary thing, you know – you can enjoy when it's working, when an orchestra is responding: we're all taking off! But it's not always the case. I tell you, when it's not, you feel terribly lonely on that podium! So you learn all these things and of course, with experience, you discover how to deal with different situations and, at the end of the day, there will always be orchestras with which you will have a relationship and others you won't.

Apart from the talent of the orchestra, or the talent of the conductor, there is an element of chemistry which comes into account. Some orchestras and conductors blend, and others don't. Any orchestra definitely has a personality, very much so! So I think the workshop idea was the best thing we could do. In America, for instance, when you work with any orchestra, you will find an assistant conductor, who is there every single rehearsal, every concert from beginning to end; it's their job to be there.

I think that this idea of taking on an assistant conductor should come just at the end of their studies, when they have spent several years studying conducting and had some training with a very good college orchestra. So, once they have managed to handle an orchestra like this, the next step is to work as an assistant conductor somewhere. But of course it is not as simple as that. They have got to go through a competition and a workshop as we did, because the higher the quality you go there are fewer and fewer orchestras. That's the way it works. When you think of the financial situation with these orchestras they hardly have the money to round off a season, so they cannot spend more on an assistant conductor.'

A number of people say that the British conductor gets on much better abroad.
'This is a rule that applies to every country. I mean, look at me! I'm also doing much better abroad than I do in France. By definition, you have an appeal abroad that you don't have in your own country.'

So, do you think that is the accent – we have to listen that bit harder to understand exactly what you want?
'Yes! I know that I owe my career only to my accent and nothing else!'

Now, I didn't mean that!
'Sorry – I'm being touchy, as always! In France we have some French conductors who have been recognised, like Michel Plasson, Jean-Claude Casadesus, Alain Lombard, and Serge Baudo. They are well respected, though some have been more successful abroad than others. In Britain there are conductors who are well established here and abroad –of course Simon Rattle, Colin Davis, Andrew Davis.

Unless somebody has something to offer there is no point in stepping up on to that podium, honestly. I am sure you agree with me. If he has something he will sell it through one channel or another, whether through regular studies, assistant conductorship, or some totally different path like mine. I have never studied conducting, which is still showing, I suppose, but I have had quite a lot of good training on the other hand, so I have done it through my own channel.'

Well, there is no one way, is there!
'No, no, especially with conducting. When it comes to instruments there are some basics you just can't escape. But with conducting, it's a totally different story. It's much broader, even though the main component has to be music. You can be a great entrepreneur, a clever man, a great intellectual, you can have a great temperament, but the best you can offer as a conductor should be music – inspiring others, communicating. Do you know that there are already half a dozen young people who have written to me saying what they have done so far and that they are now stuck and don't know what to do. I'm telling them that, hopefully, we will have another workshop here leading into another position as assistant and we will let them know when we have our next competition.'

I understand that, in Finland, Panula will talk to some students for a few hours in the sauna and assess whether they have the makings of a conductor or not.
'That's the psychological approach. Their character and personality have to be exploited as far as possible on musical grounds. If someone steps on to the podium with personality, but he is expressing views which have no real connection with the music, then an orchestra will tell pretty soon.'

Well, you have ninety minds in front of you.
'You have ninety minds but we have one thing in common and that is music. You can say we all have different approaches, but that is what the conductor must do, to mould it in such a way that there will be a final musical result out of the ninety people.'

Or at least the majority on your side?
'Yes! I like the way you said 'or the majority – as many as you can!' Sometimes you have to give in. I admit that there is a school

of conductors who do it with a sheer intellectual and controlled approach; this is of course possible. I cannot do it that way because this is not me. I have to express it physically and I like the orchestra to respond physical, too. A conductor will receive the waves from the orchestra and you conduct accordingly. Going from one orchestra to another is very much like driving different cars. There is a time in response and reactions and depending on countries, orchestras behave in a different way. A German or French orchestra are both much heavier to drive. I recently did a Franck symphony with a German orchestra, and what a real depth of sound they produced. But then, when you want to move....gosh! You can't! So you must adapt, because otherwise you create a confrontation.'

So you meet them half-way?
'That's it! That is it!'

CODA

It has surely become clear that a conductor's training is endless, like the escalators rising from the underground tube station: once you get to the end of one stairway, you walk to another and start again, only this time you do not reach the ground level, but go soaring off into the stratosphere. It is from these dizzy heights that orchestras and audiences want to be inspired; half-way up the staircase is just not good enough.

The conducting courses have to be justified; they feel under pressure all the time, just because there is no end product for sale – in a manner of speaking.

This could be an opportunity for Britain to excel and lead the way for orchestral life in the future. There is no point, in my mind, in having a healthy department in the conservatoires for woodwind and percussion, for example, and no concerted effort to raise the standard at the pinnacle of power, that is, the music director or conductor. On the other hand, perhaps the conservatoires here have assessed the situation correctly; perhaps the heyday of the figurehead is over and orchestras can manage without some important sounding name on the programme. With the finances of the whole musical scene, perhaps the vast sum of money paid to certain conductors per concert is no longer a viable proposition and shouldn't be encouraged in any shape or form. The estimated value of Karajan's estate at his death was conservatively put at £163 million. The public should not be expected to sustain this sort of luxury, surely?

Rather than postgraduate courses, why is it not possible to study the fundamentals at a much earlier stage, and leave the psychological and deeper studies for these final years of maturity? Yielding a baton is something that many musicians are expected to be able to do at a moment's notice - organizing a chamber group, a school or amateur orchestra, a choir, a brass band, a jazz band, and probably many more. Surely this aspect is such an important part of our musical training - it should be an essential aspect of any music qualification at a college or university. As a knock on effect the whole standard of directing ensembles all over the country would improve, the status of the conductor trainers would be raised, the awareness inside the college of such a faculty would also be given a kick start. If we can only allow two or three years for this specialisation, then let us please make the most of the time available.

If we supposed that the conservatoires did begin to take things more seriously and that conductors were getting a fair crack of the whip, then what would the next stage be? The finalists in the BBC workshop all agreed on one particular thing – lack of practice in a professional situation meant a valuable loss in experience. They can work with the college symphony orchestra every day of the week for a year, but they might only be discussing tempi, dynamics, bowings, questions of balance. All essential, no doubt, but far removed from the real world of group psychology: the One in charge of many, the One capturing the imagination of many, and the One having enough background insight into the pieces to win the respect and authority that goes with it.

When young conductors come to watch and learn from the rehearsal techniques of others on the podium, they would learn far more from a vantage spot within the orchestra, rather than from the audience. In fact, the players might welcome the opportunity to discuss certain aspects of professional playing with the students; this could be a two-way process. Now I understand that this might be unnerving for the main conductor, who wants to appear faultless, but, in time, this could be an acceptable way forward. In fact, the whole essence of standing in front of a professional orchestra for the first time, the thrill and panic that it must hold for the contestants, this might be less frightening if the opposing parties had met before. We tend to think of the conductor as being all-powerful, but there has been a shift of emphasis away from the fierce controller, and it might be now that the orchestra, sticking together as a solid group, is more frightening to the person on the rostrum than would ever have seemed possible a few years ago. The players themselves might not yet be aware of this hidden power, and perhaps don't realise that they can appear threatening to the lonely figure high on his podium.

A solution to this might be inviting small groups from the professional orchestras into the colleges to do a session with the young conductors on their own territory, so that it would not be as daunting (or as expensive) as the large concert hall and a full 100 piece band. Yes, the conductors do need help and experience, but is that like asking a newly qualified driver to ride safely round the grand prix track at breath-taking speeds?

Very few conductors have had as easy ride to the podium. Karajan is remembered for the business deals, cars, planes, jet flights and lucrative deals on recordings etc., and left a very large estate, but even he had to start somewhere. He decided to form a group of players that would spend eight hours a day on the opera that was due to be performed, one conducting, four playing the piano, two or three singing the choir and solo parts, etc. Then they all went to the opera to see it performed from the fourth gallery , discussing it later over a glass of beer, learning seventy operas in that fashion before he left. He even listened to Toscanini's rehearsals of 'Falstaff' for the Salzburg Festival hidden behind the organ, as rehearsals were closed to the public. His first gig with a professional orchestra was in 1929 in Salzburg, when he actually hired the Mozarteum orchestra at his own expense. His job of first kapellmeister in the small town of Ulm had a monthly salary of £10. Yet he stayed there five years with a 24 member orchestra with its four first violins and a six metre stage. He even carried instruments round in a wheelbarrow from the theatre to the restaurant where they rehearsed![27]

Mackerras relates how he had to take over a performance of 'Cavalleria Rusticana' and 'Pagliacci' at extremely short when one of the principal conductors in the Sadler's Wells company, Michael Mudie, became ill. 'Sometimes you have to be able to conduct without a rehearsal. When you can do that, you're on your way.'

Sir Thomas Beecham, who created the London Philharmonic and the Royal Philharmonic Orchestras had the backing of his father in St Helens. In 1899, Sir Joseph Beecham engaged Hans Richter and the Hallé for the inaugural concert of St

---

[27] Matheopoulos 246-248

Helens new town hall. At the last minute, Richter was unable to appear, so the 20 yr old, self taught Beecham took his place conducting Beethoven 5, Tchaikovsky 6, Wagner Preludes to 'Tannhäuser' and 'Meistersinger' - all from memory and with no rehearsal.[28]

So, there has never been one direct route to the podium in the past, and who knows what the future for orchestras will be, let alone their conductors? The enthusiasm by the youth in Venezuela with El Sistema shows that the artistic side of our nature should have a prominent place in our everyday lives. Musicians have always had to fight for their existence and the success of orchestras in the future lies not only in the quality of their players but in the inspiration they receive from the podium. It is this symbiosis that is so essential to maintain a healthy balance between conductors and players. The audience must feel involved and uplifted. If there is no communication there is no justification for the concert taking place at all. Leonard Bernstein was able to put this into words succinctly:

'And the reason why I love conducting is that I love the people I conduct, and I love the people for whom we play. It's a great love affair, what's going on out there. But it's a mystery because, whatever happens, it's the most potent love affair you can have in your life. And it involves over a hundred people. It's incredible when you have over a hundred people breathing together, pulsing together. It's almost unbearable at times....when they are in the mood and this special something happens.

I love it, because you make the musicians forget that they are playing in a professional orchestra and why they ever wanted to join it in the first place - because they loved music too.' [29]

---

[28] Bowen 71,185
[29] Matheopoulos, 10

178

PHOTOGRAPHS AND DESIGN

Front cover-
> Photo of Sir Edward Downes CBE, taken by Tom
> Bangbala
> Design by Anthony Jay

Back Cover-
> Photo of Pam Jay, taken by Andrew Price
> Design by Anthony Jay

Photos by TOM BANGBALA
> Sir Andrew Davis CBE
> Sir Charles Mackerras CBE
> Günther Herbig
> Sir Mark Elder CBE
> Harry Christophers
> Gianandrea Noseda
> Yan Pascal Tortelier and Jean Yves Thibaubet
> Vassily Sinaisky
> Sir Edward Downes CBE

Photos by ANDREW PRICE
> Pam Jay
> Vassily Sinaisky and Nigel Jay on the Great Wall of China.
> Tecwyn Evans during the performance of the celebration of
> the moon landing anniversary
> H.K.Gruber and James Macmillan CBE in the Green Room

Photo by JOHN WADE.
> Sir Edward and Lady Downes in Oman.

BIBLIOGRAPHY

Many thanks to the following authors and publishers for giving their permissions to quote:

Boonschaft, Peter Loel. "Teaching Music with Passion." By permission of Meredith Music Publication, 2002.

Boult, Adrian C. "A Handbook on the Technique of Conducting." By permission of Music Sales Limited.

Bowen, Jose Antonio. "The Cambridge Companion to Conducting, 2003. By permission of Cambridge University Press.

Matheopoulos, Helena. "Maestro." By permission of Harper Collins.

Orr, Deborah. By permission of Deborah Orr and The Independent.

Rudolf, Max. "The Grammar of Conducting." Second Edition, New York. G.Schirmer Inc., 1980. By permission of Cengage Learning.

Scherchen, Hermann "Handbook of Conducting." By permission of Oxford University Press and by permission of Oxford University Press, Inc.

Schuller, Gunther from "The Complete Conductor." By permission of Oxford University Press and by permission of Oxford University Press, Inc.

Younghusband, Jan. "Orchestra." By permission of Channel 4 Rights.

Many thanks to:

**THE MANCHESTER
MUSICAL HERITAGE TRUST**

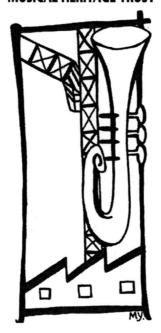

The Ida Carroll Trust
(In Association with the Manchester Musical Heritage Trust)

LaVergne, TN USA
18 June 2010
186587LV00004B/8/P